CONNECT & COLOR

WILD ANIMALS

Racehorse Publishing books may be purchased in bulk at special discounts for sales promotion, corporate gifts, fund-raising, or educational purposes. Special editions can also be created to specifications. For details, contact the Special Sales Department, Skyhorse Publishing, 307 West 36th Street, 11th Floor, New York, NY 10018 or info@skyhorsepublishing.com.

Racehorse Publishing™ is a pending trademark of Skyhorse Publishing, Inc.®, a Delaware corporation.

Visit our website at www.skyhorsepublishing.com.

10 9 8 7 6 5 4 3 2 1

Cover and interior artwork by Jessica Mazurkiewicz
Art Assistant: Lucy Richmond

Print ISBN: 978-1-944686-75-8

Printed in the United States of America

CONNECT & COLOR

WILD ANIMALS

An Intricate Coloring and Dot-to-Dot Book

Jessica Mazurkiewicz

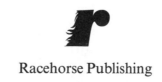

Racehorse Publishing

DOT-TO-DOT GUIDE

○ = Start

◆ = Finish

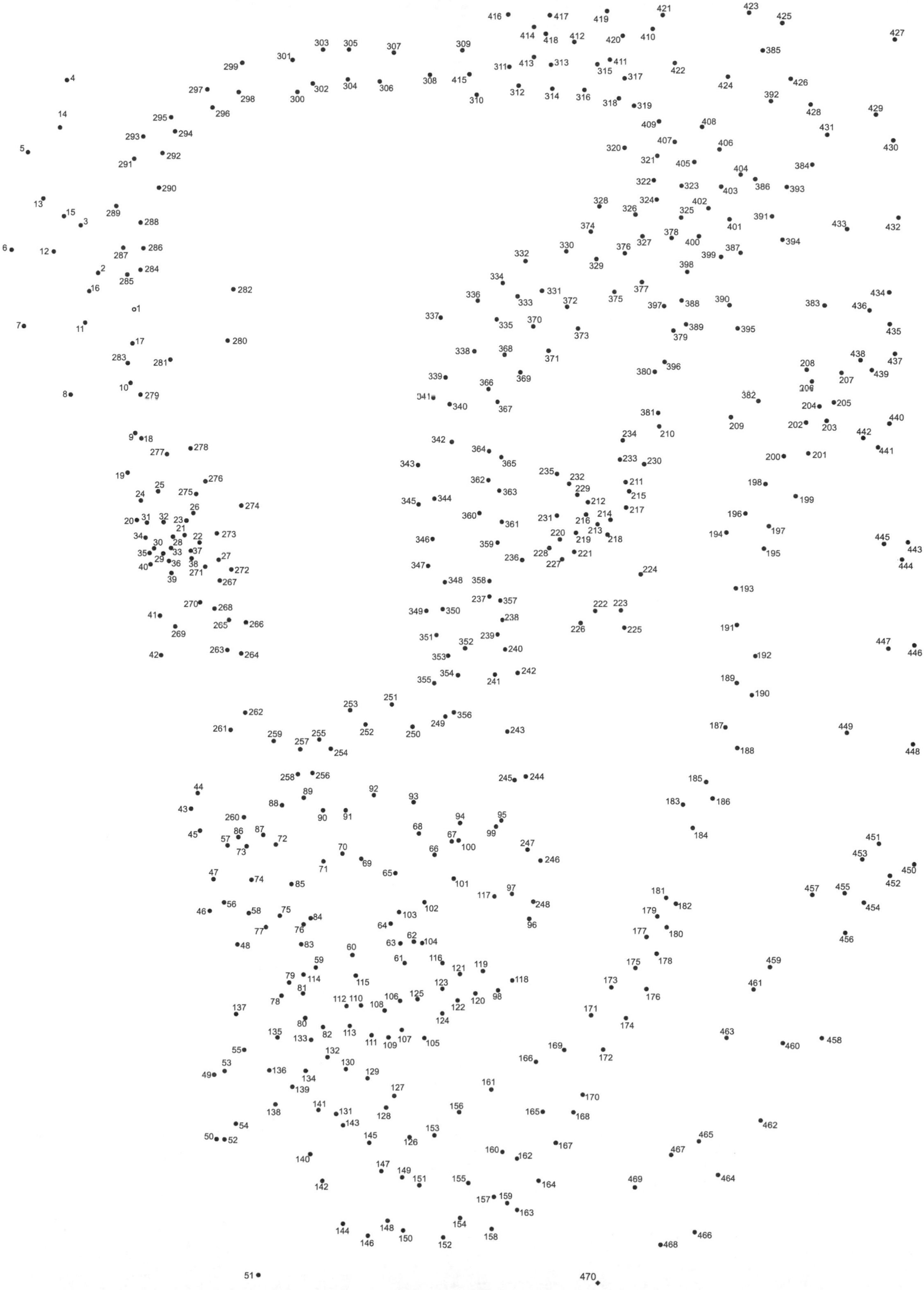

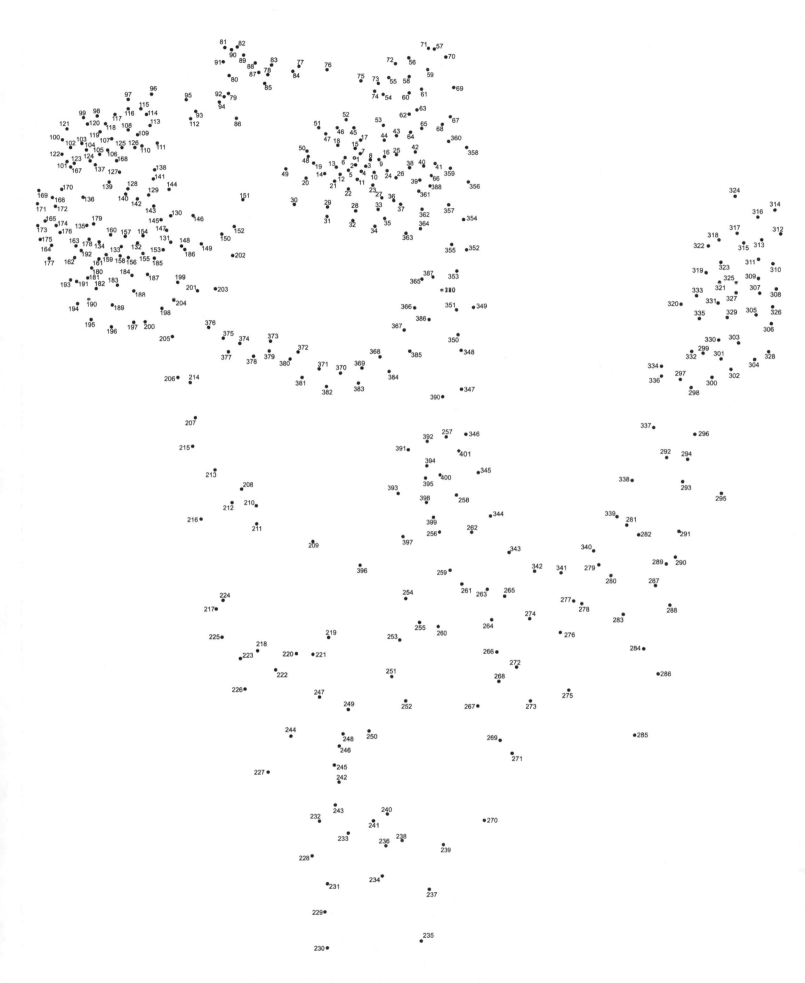

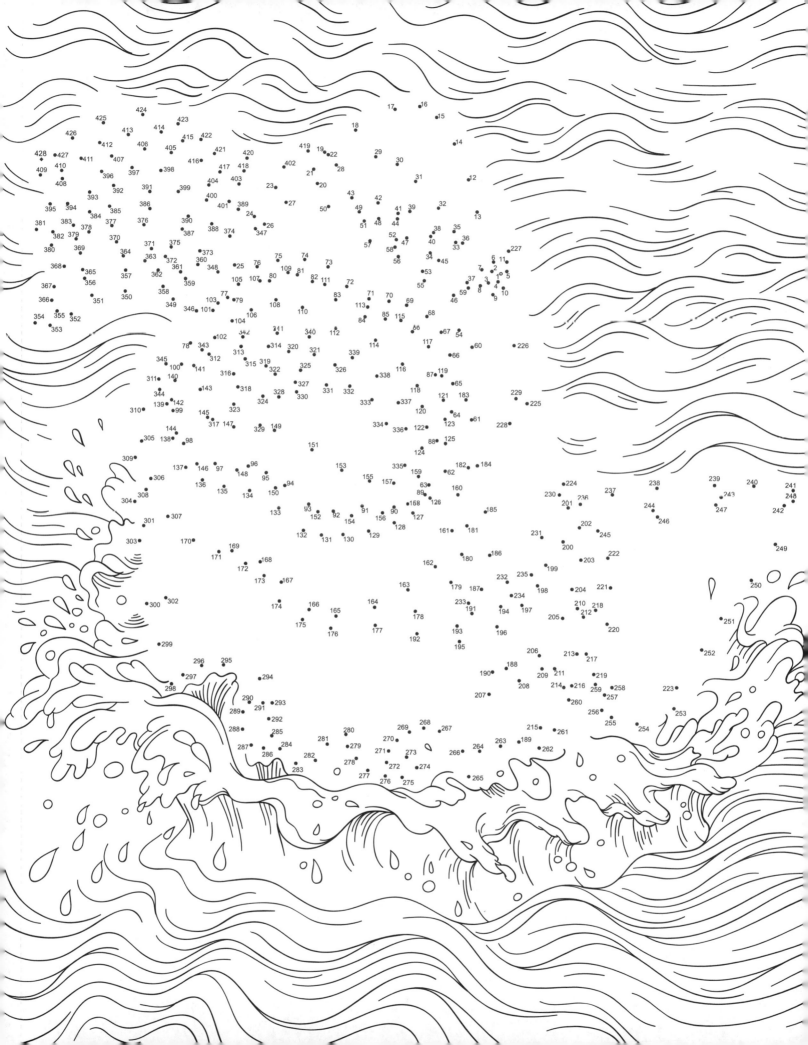

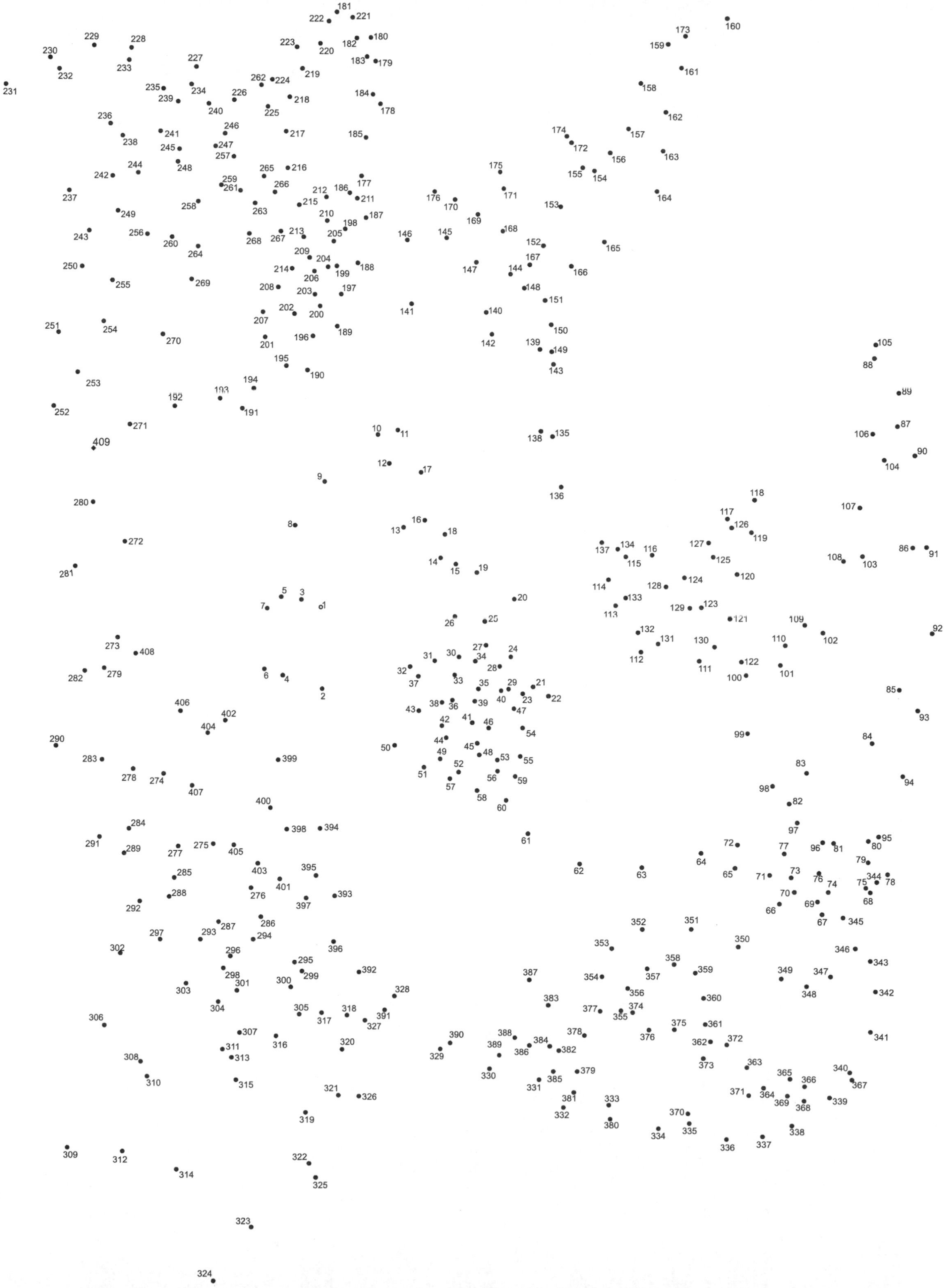

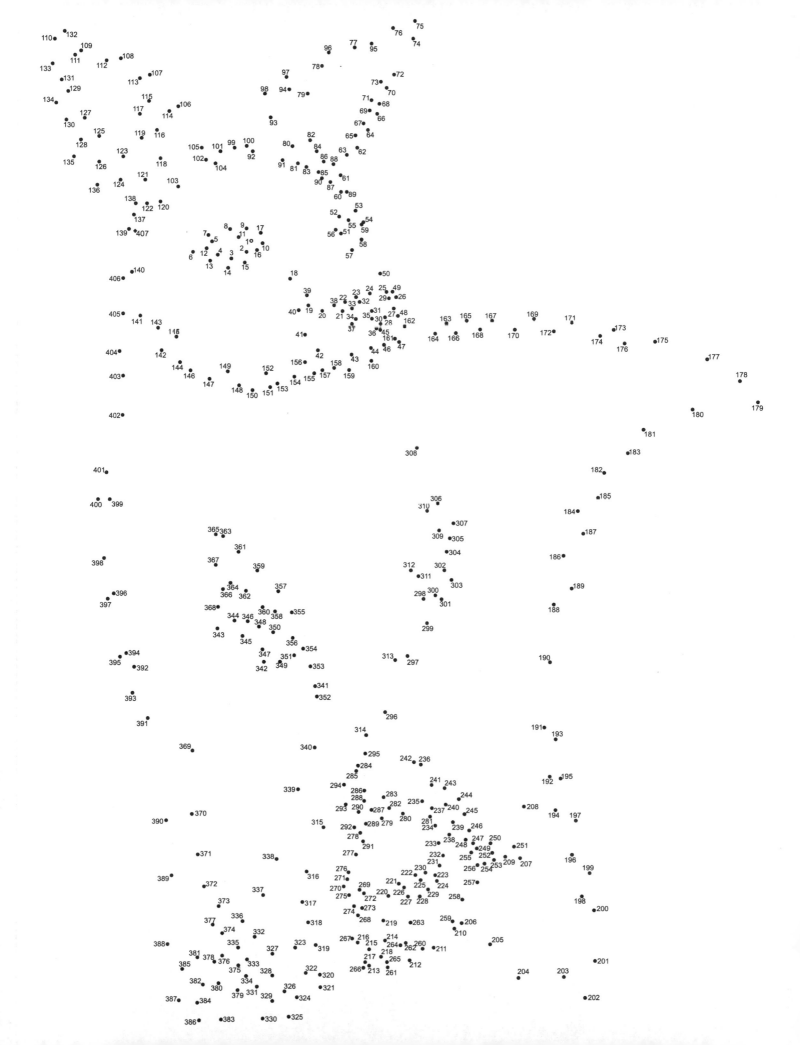

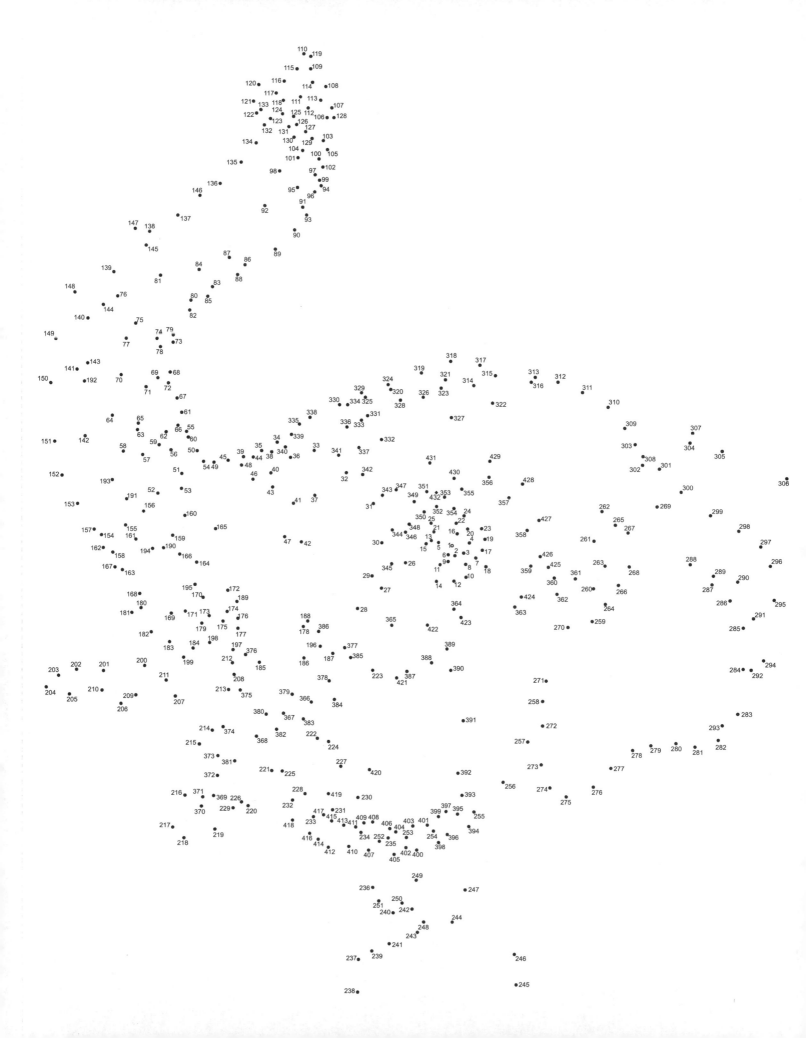

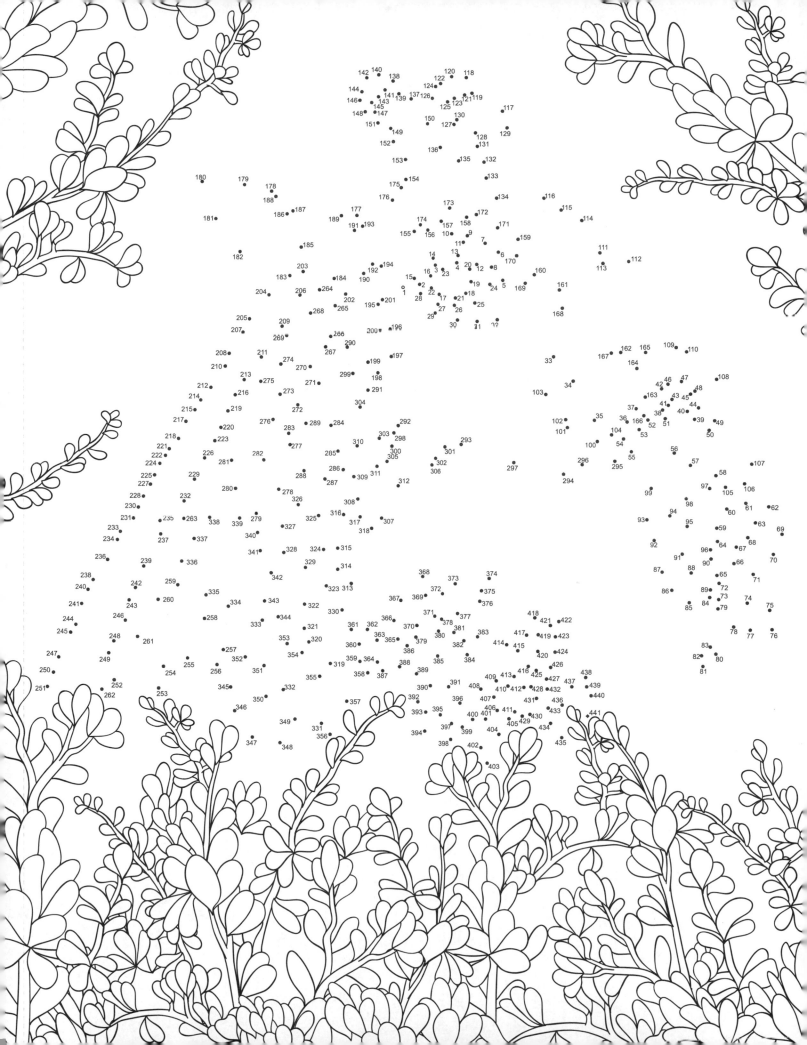

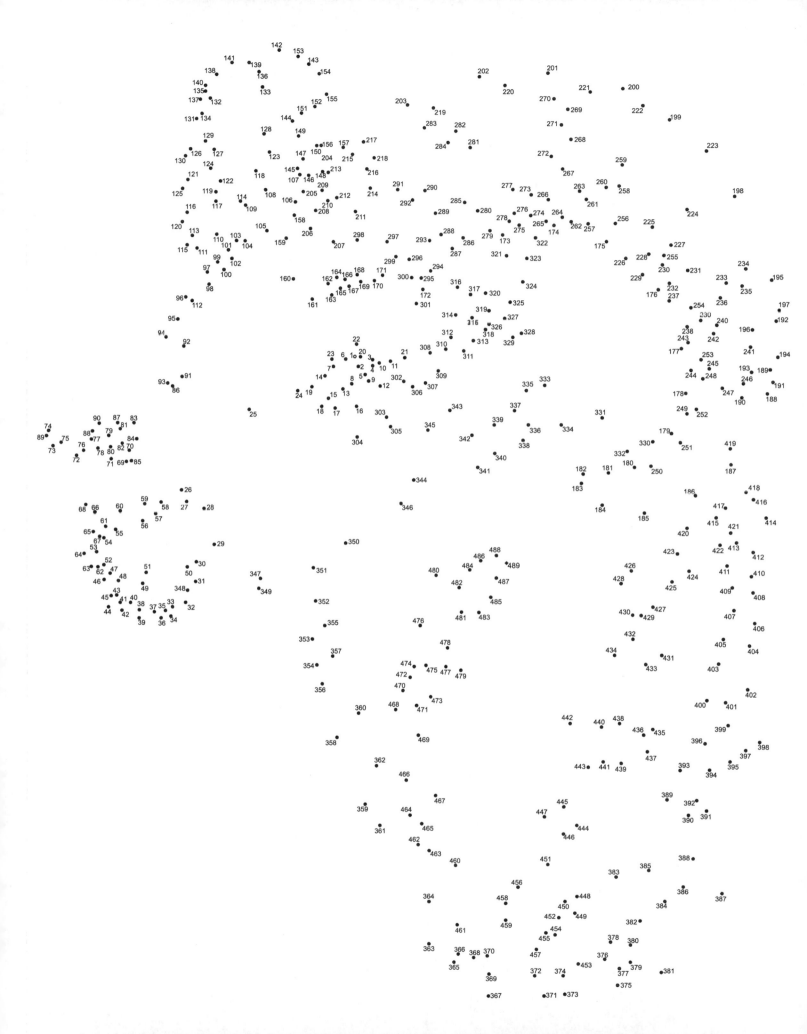

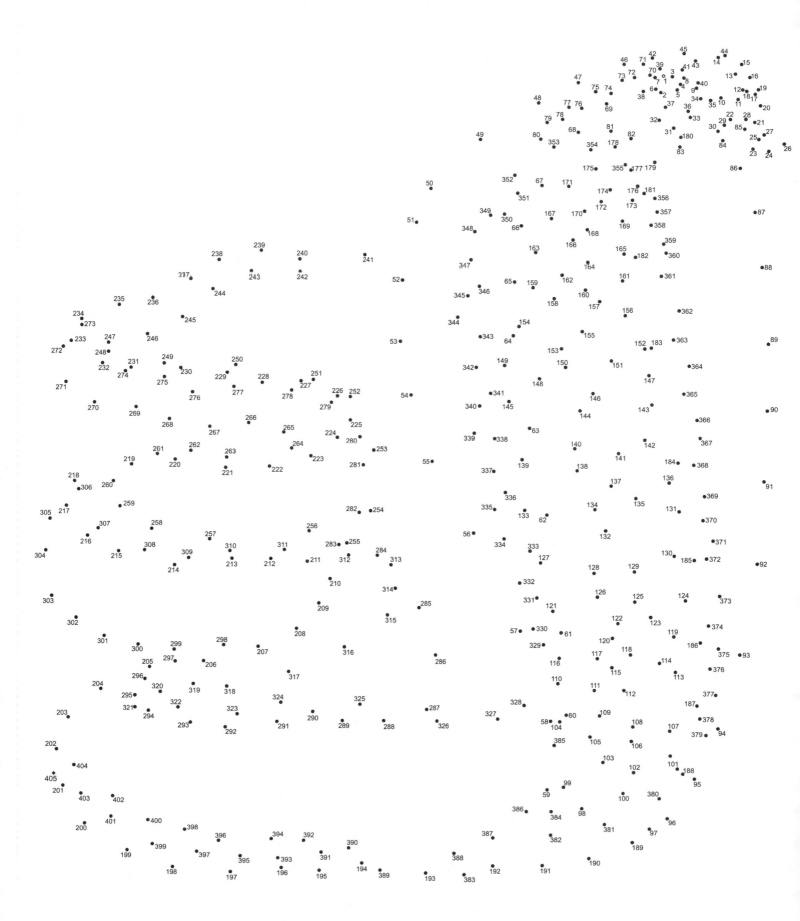

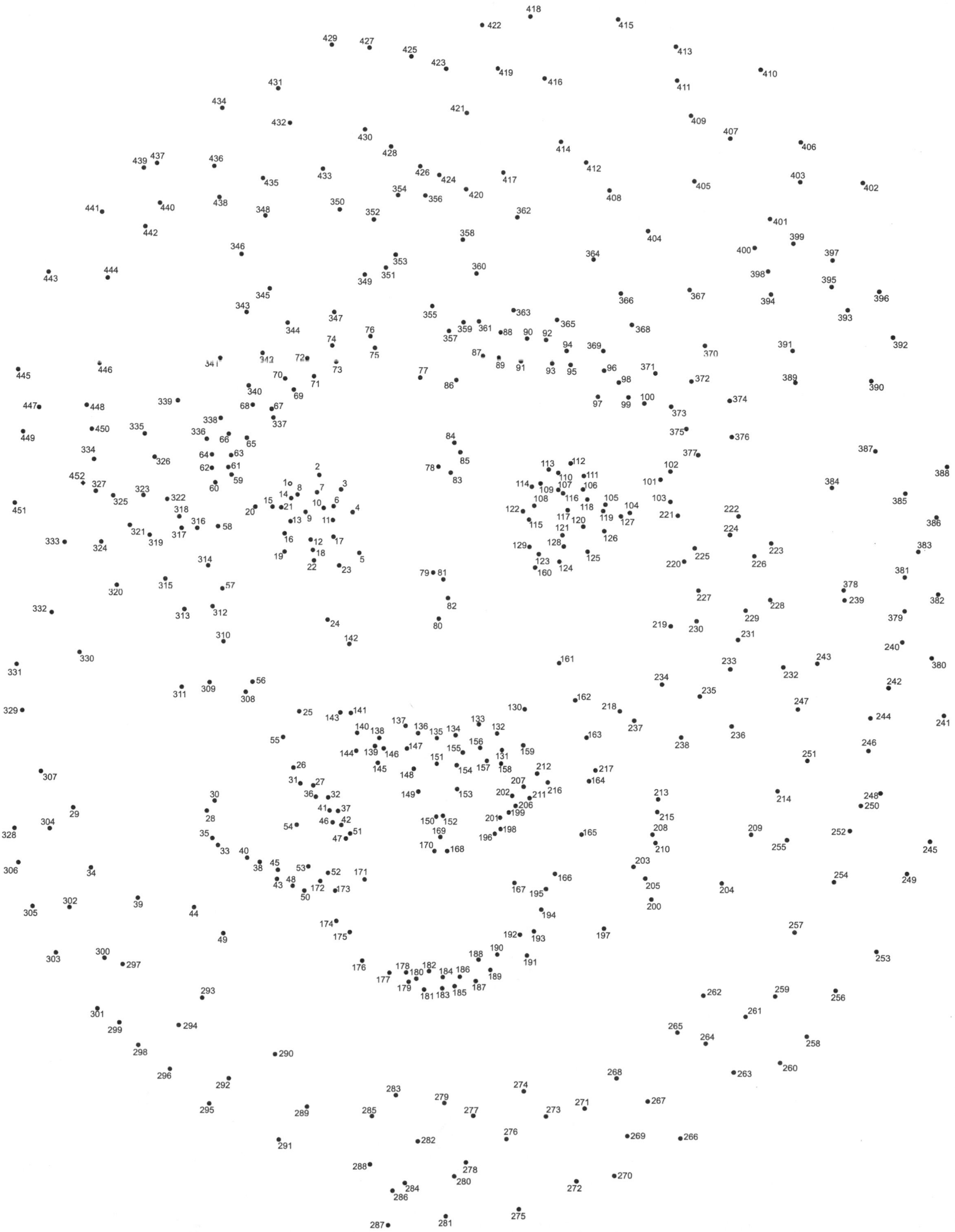

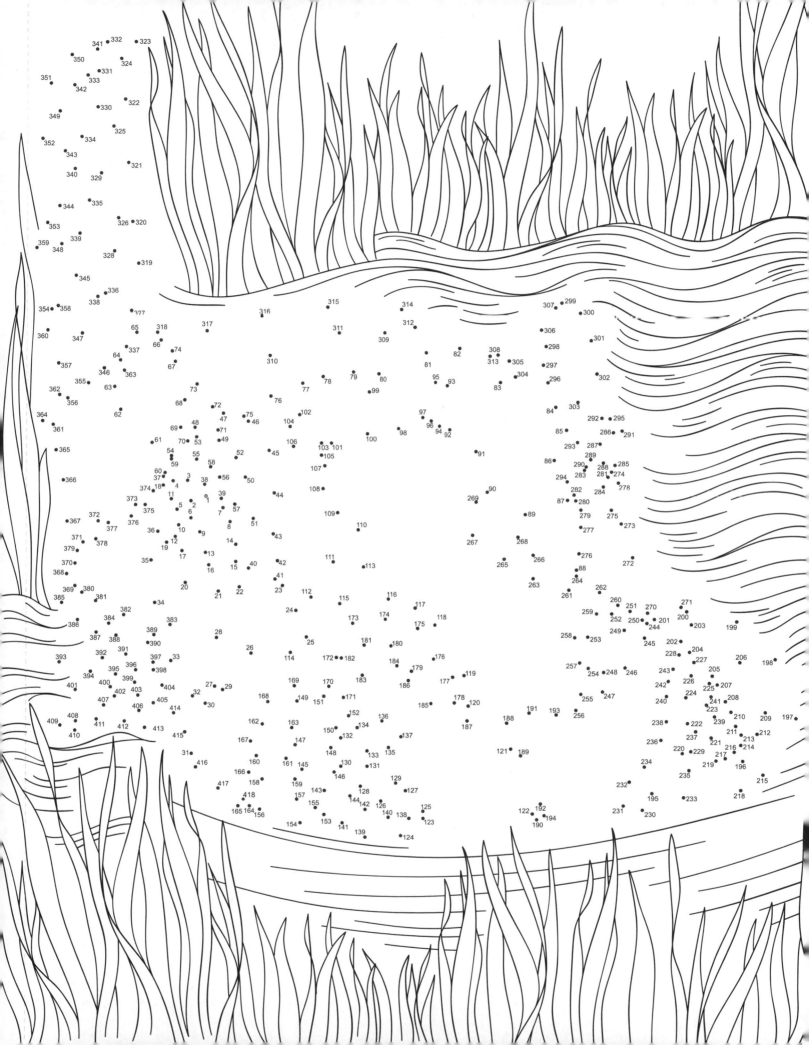

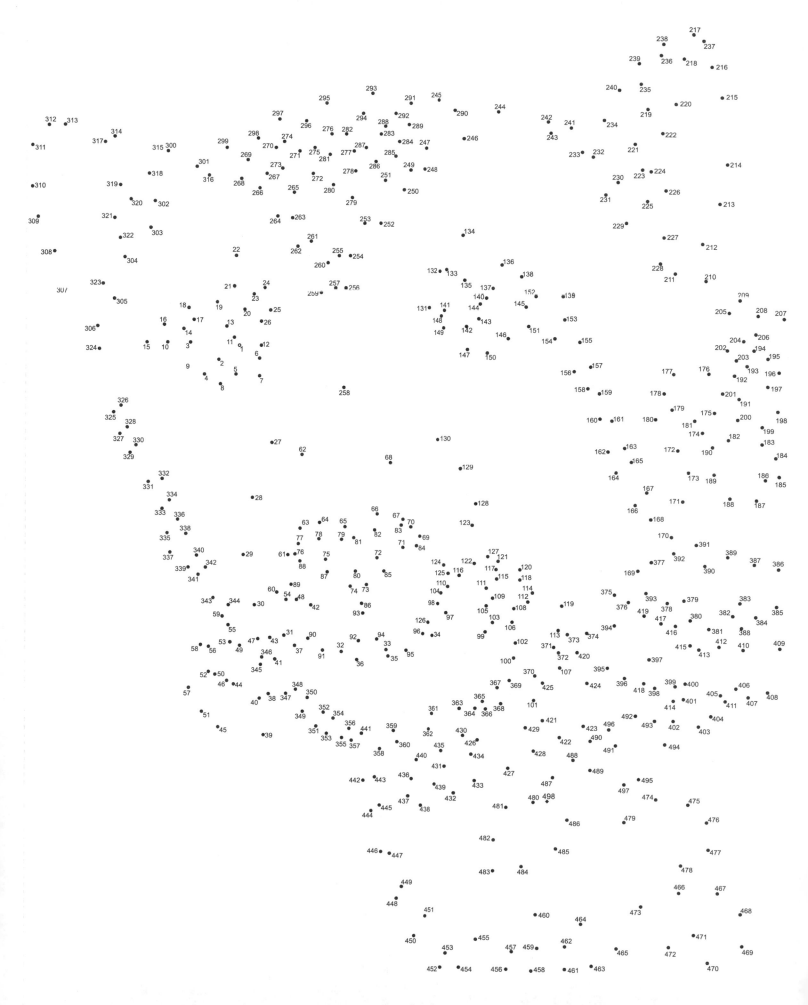

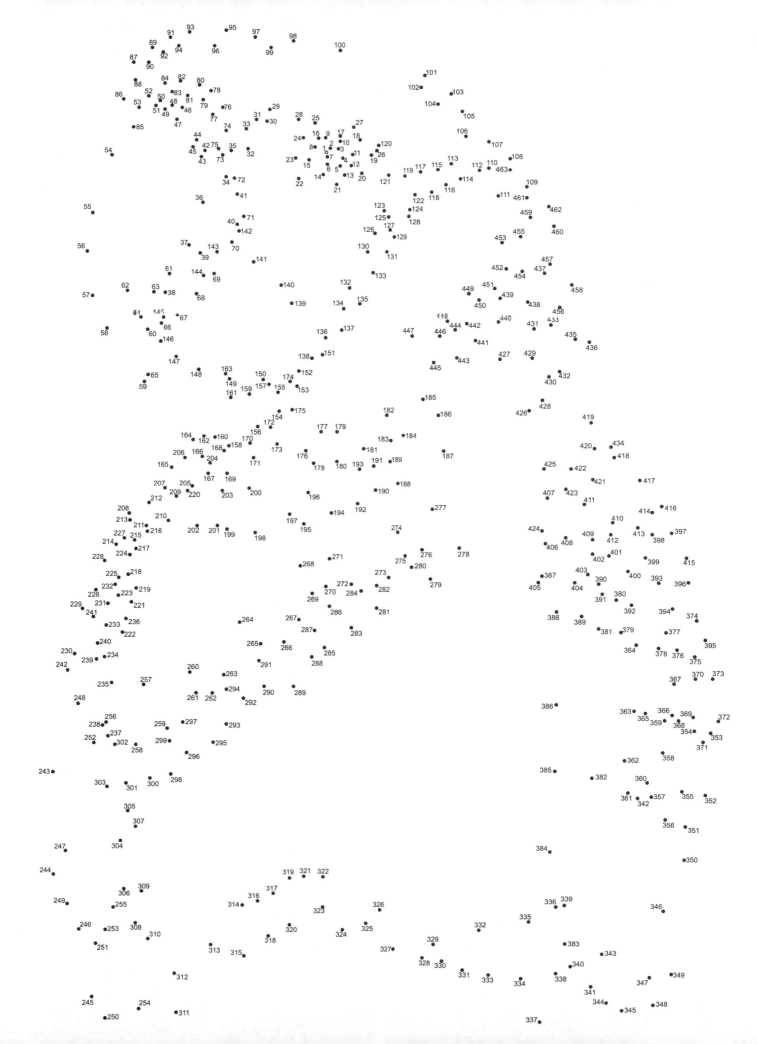

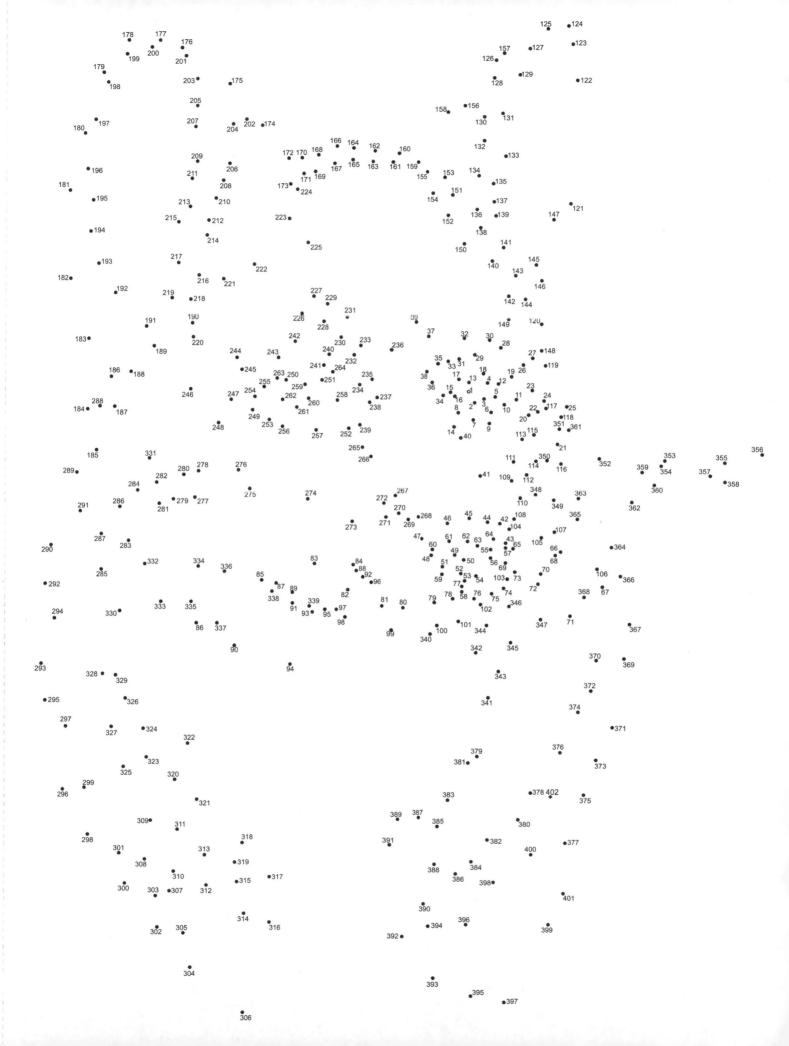

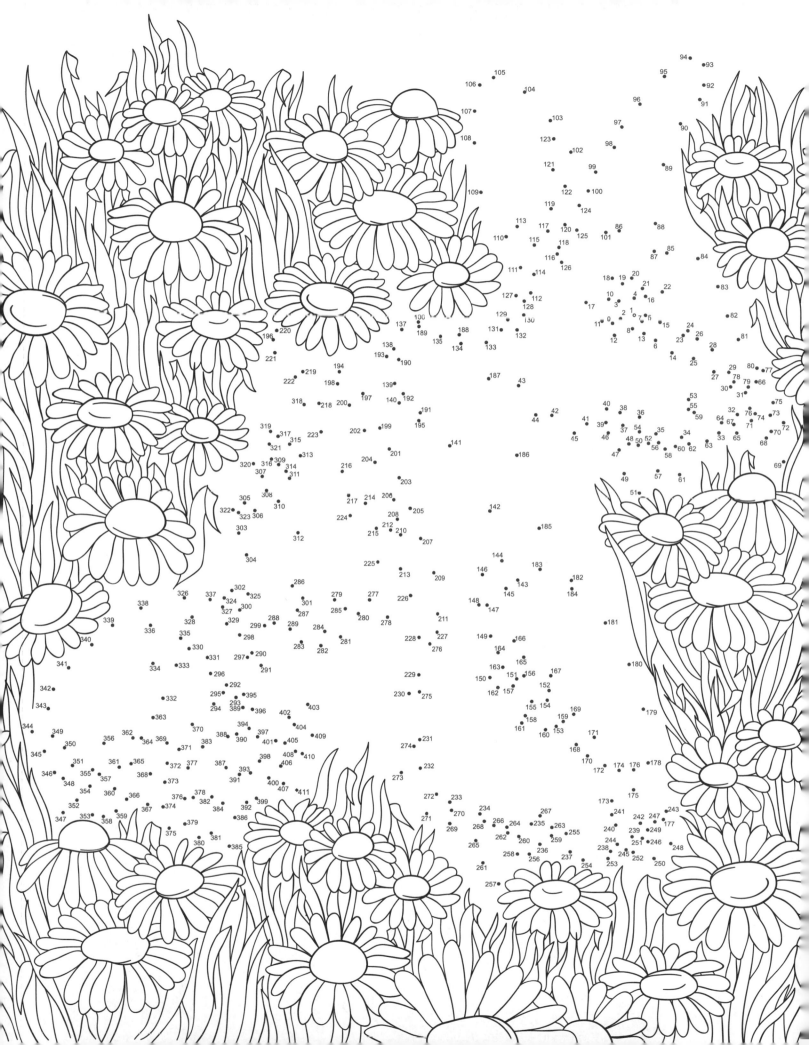

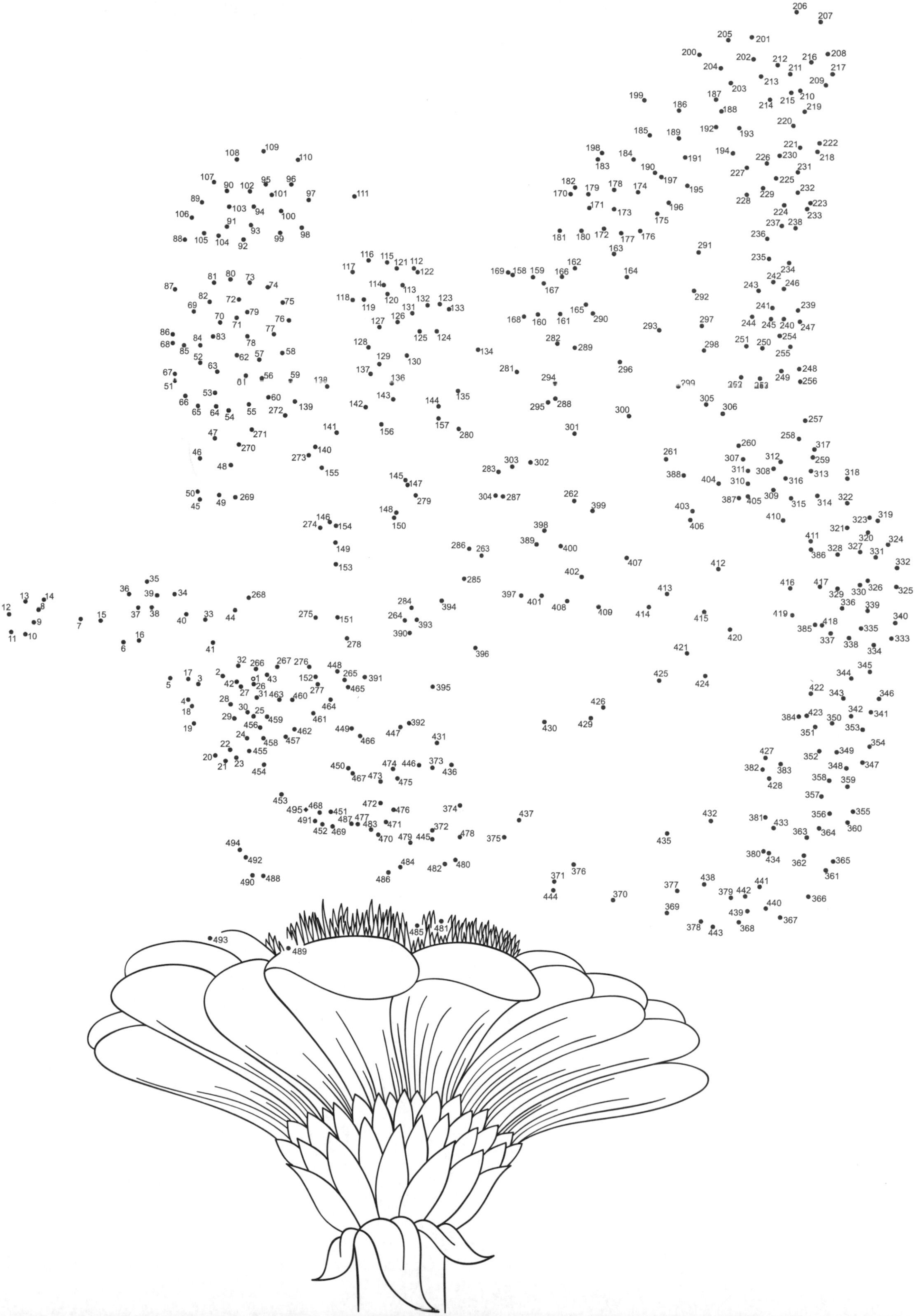

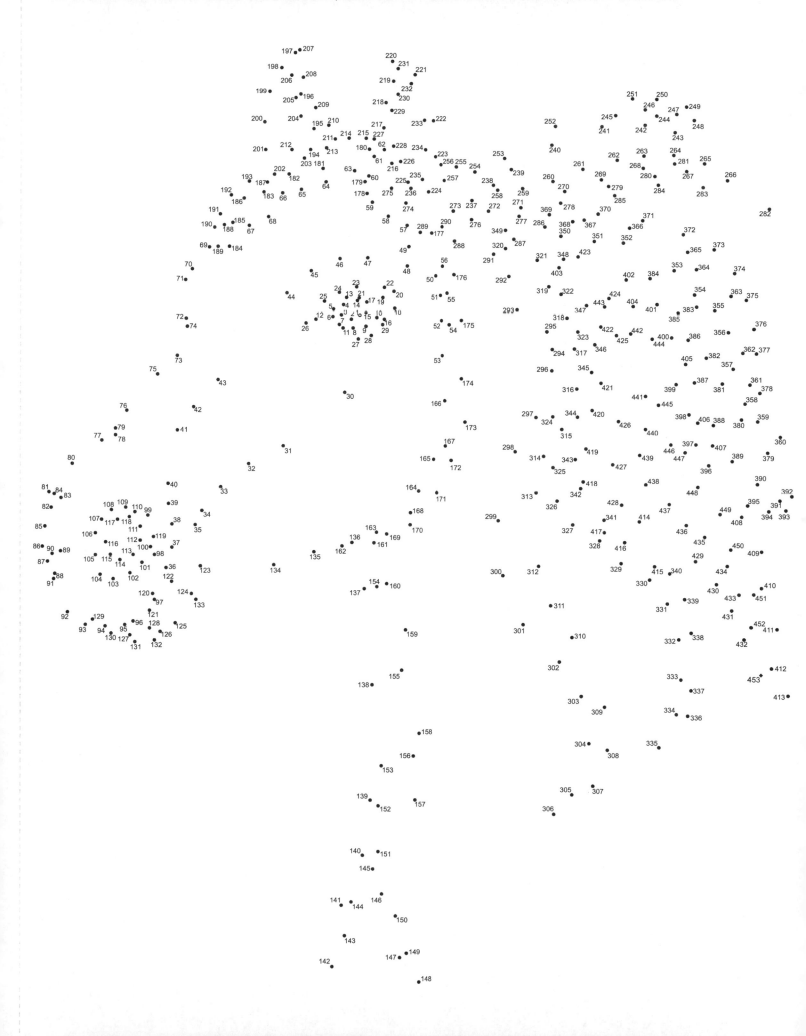

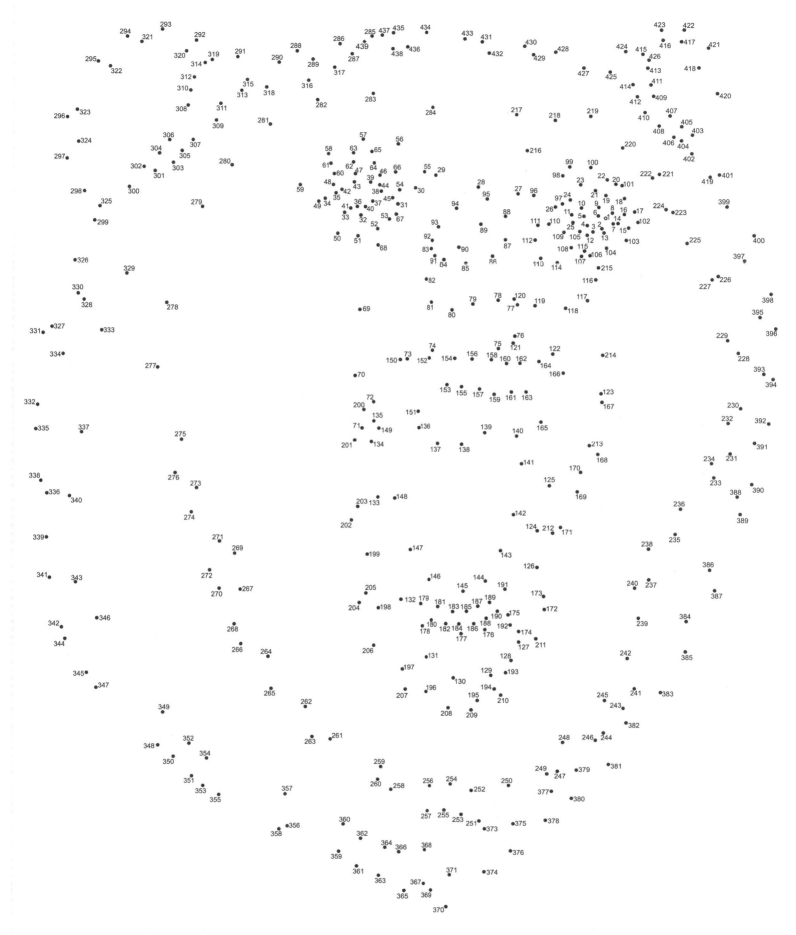

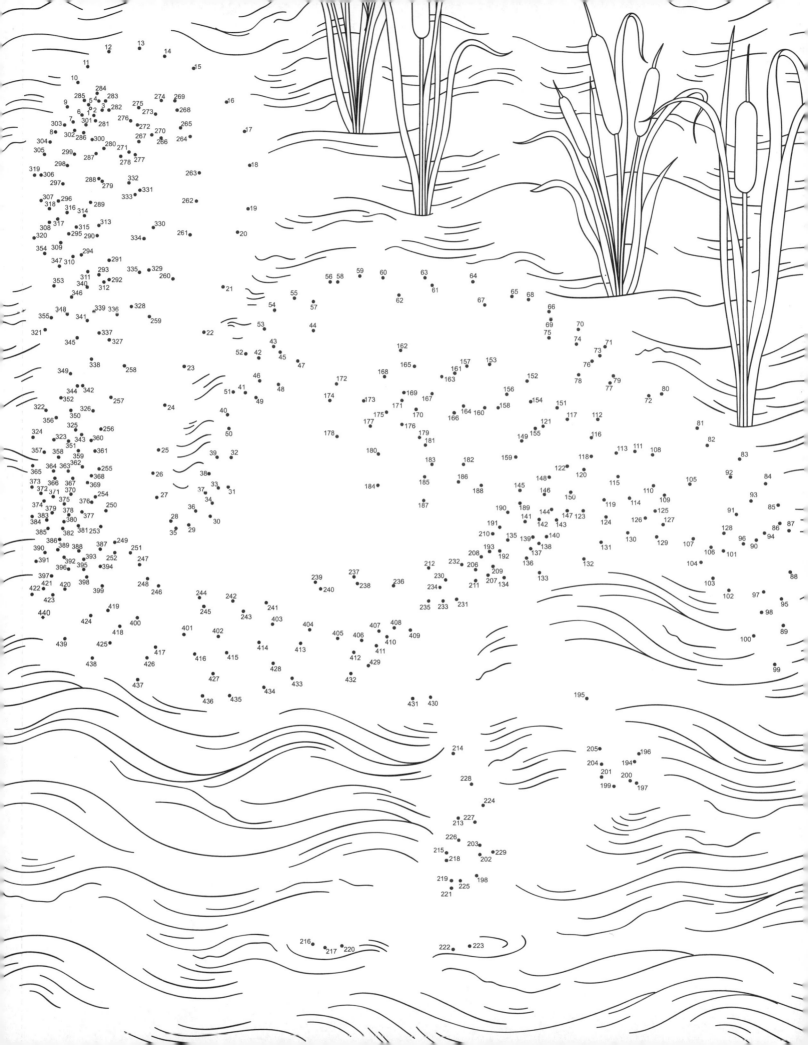

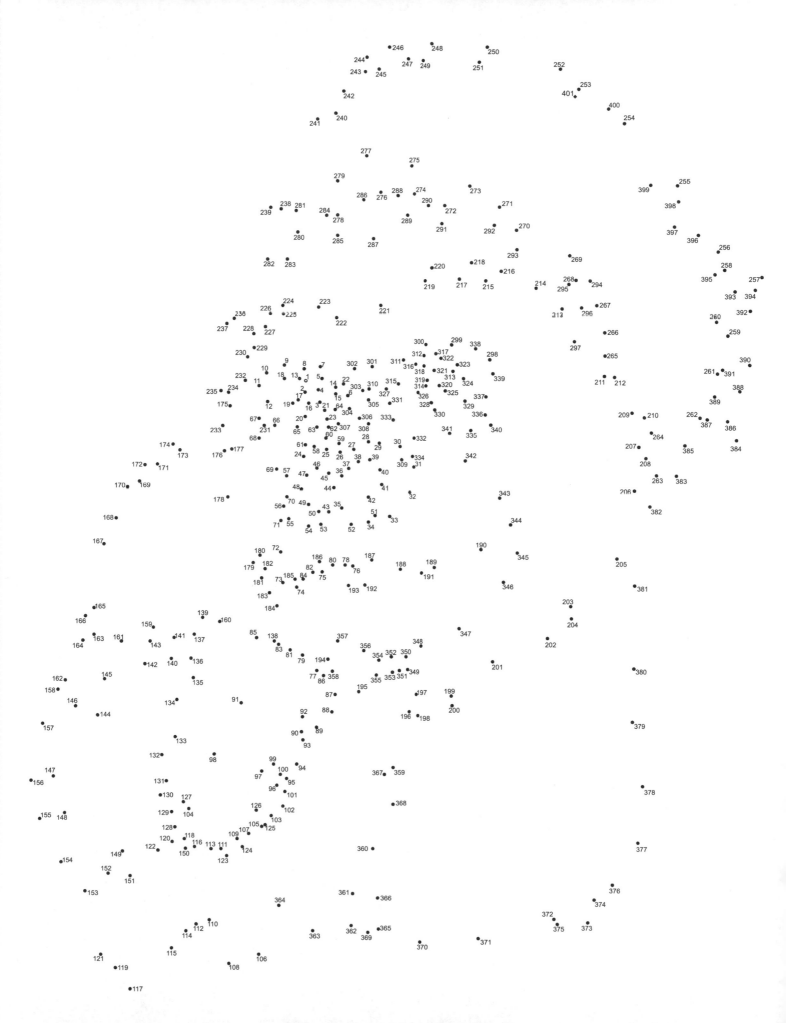

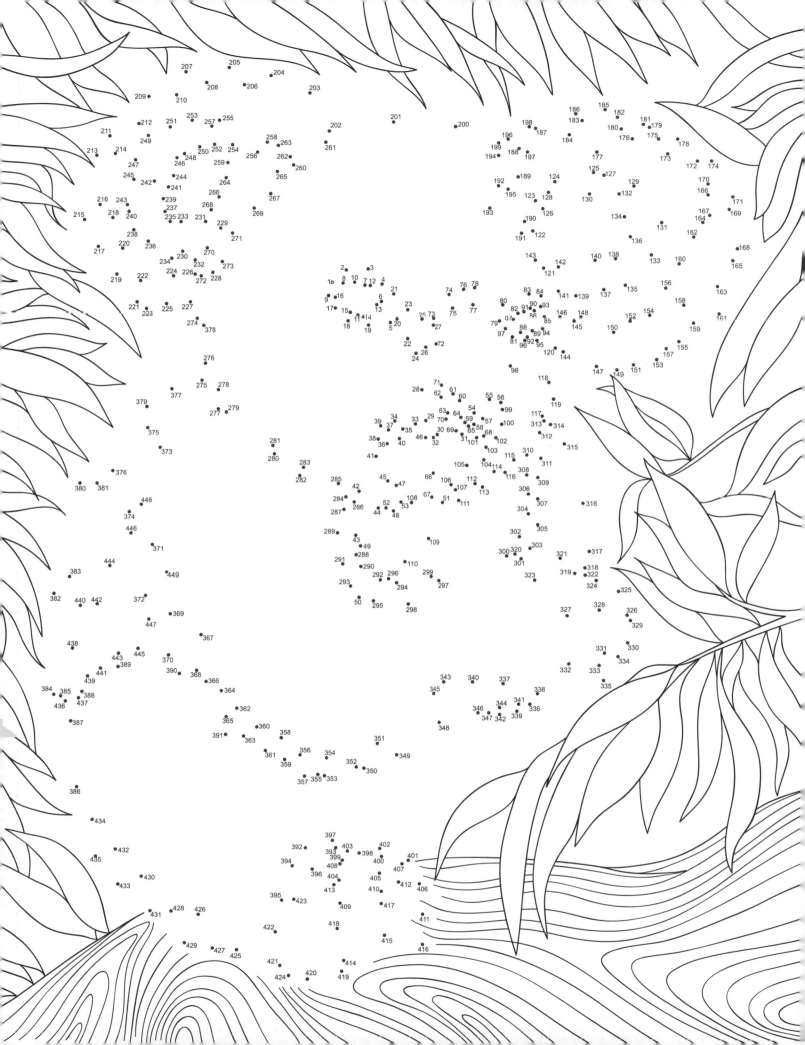

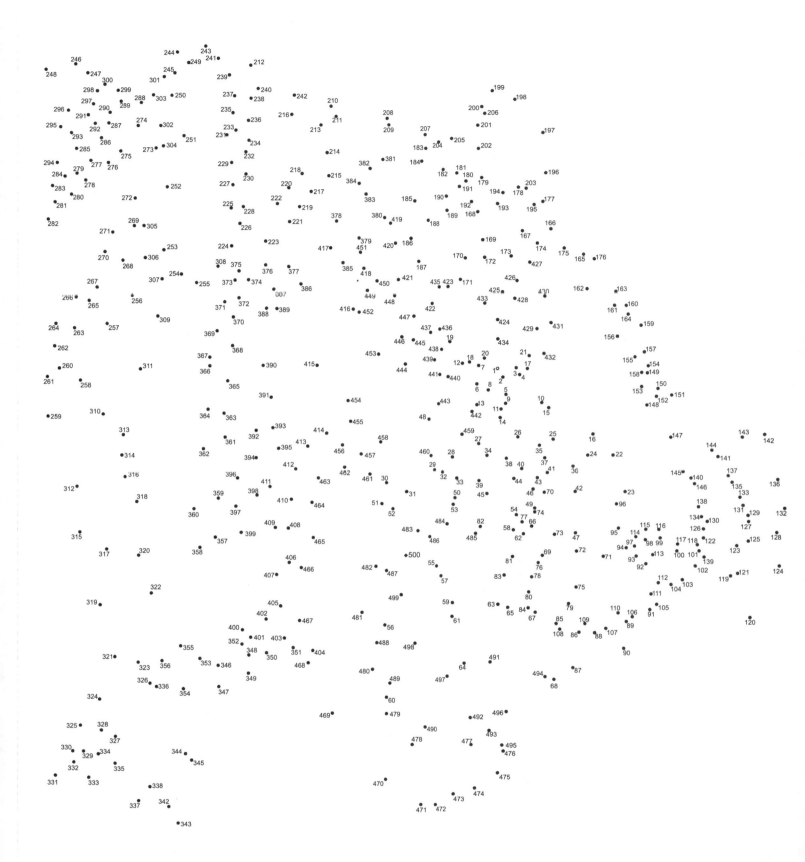

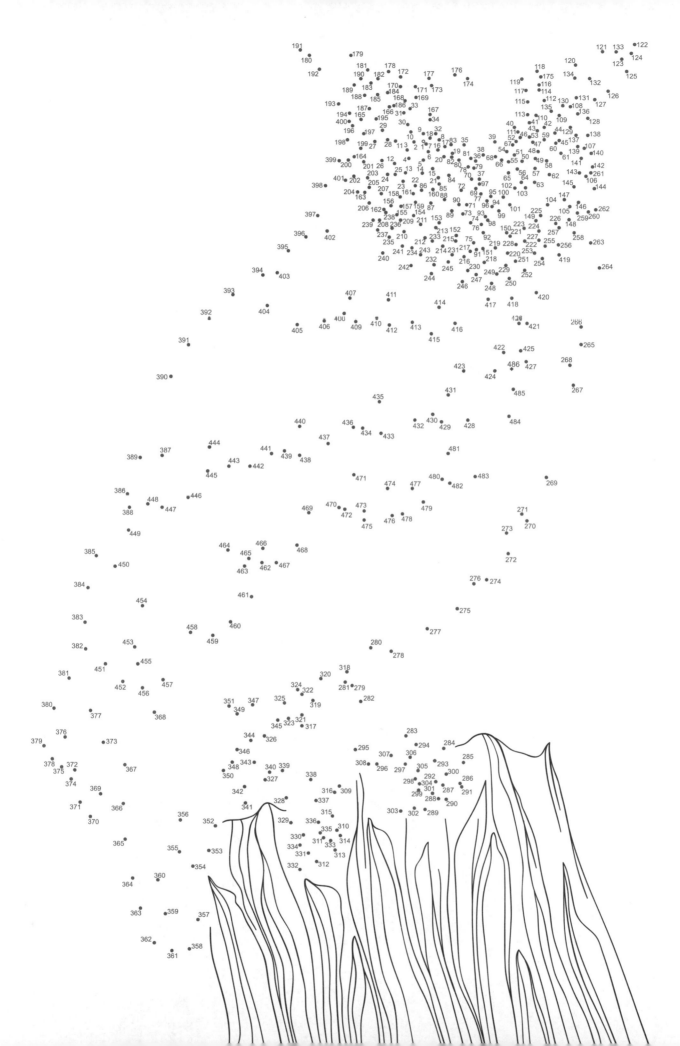

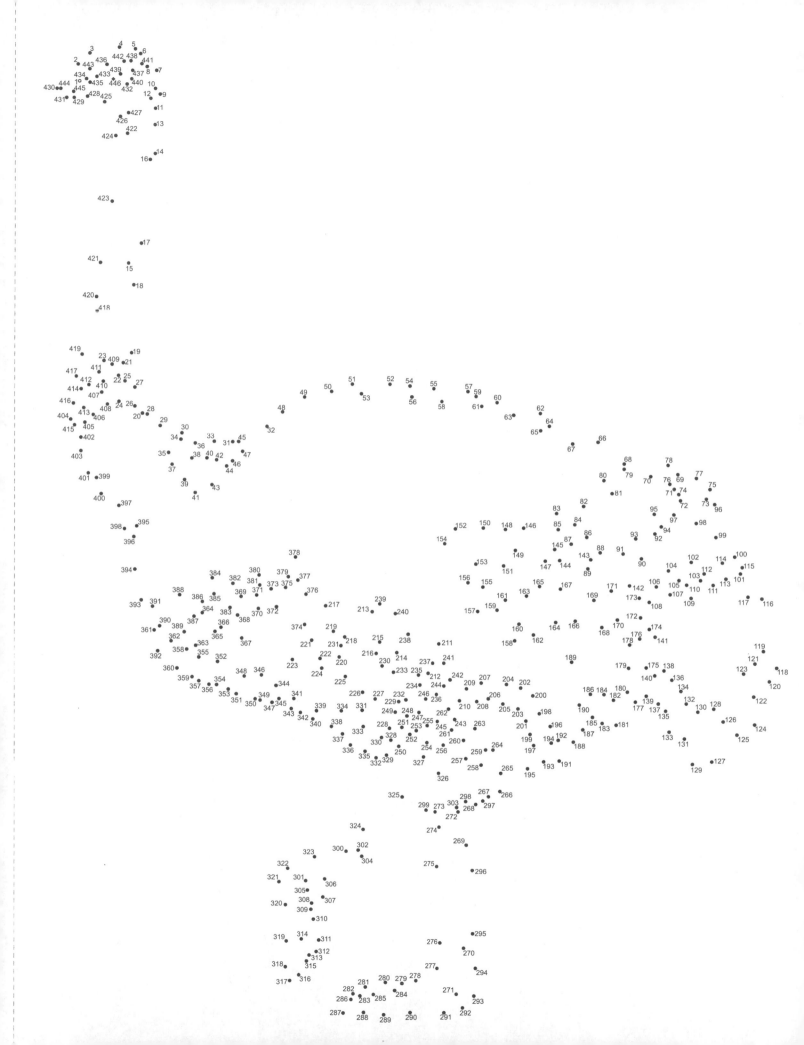

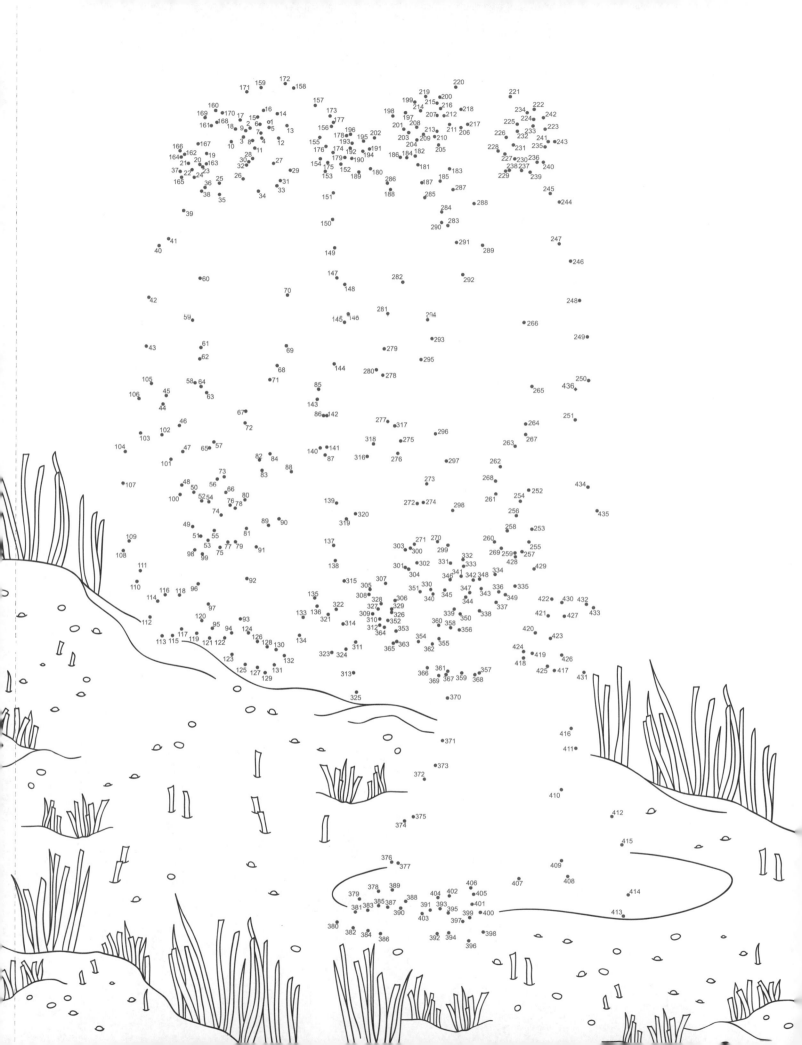

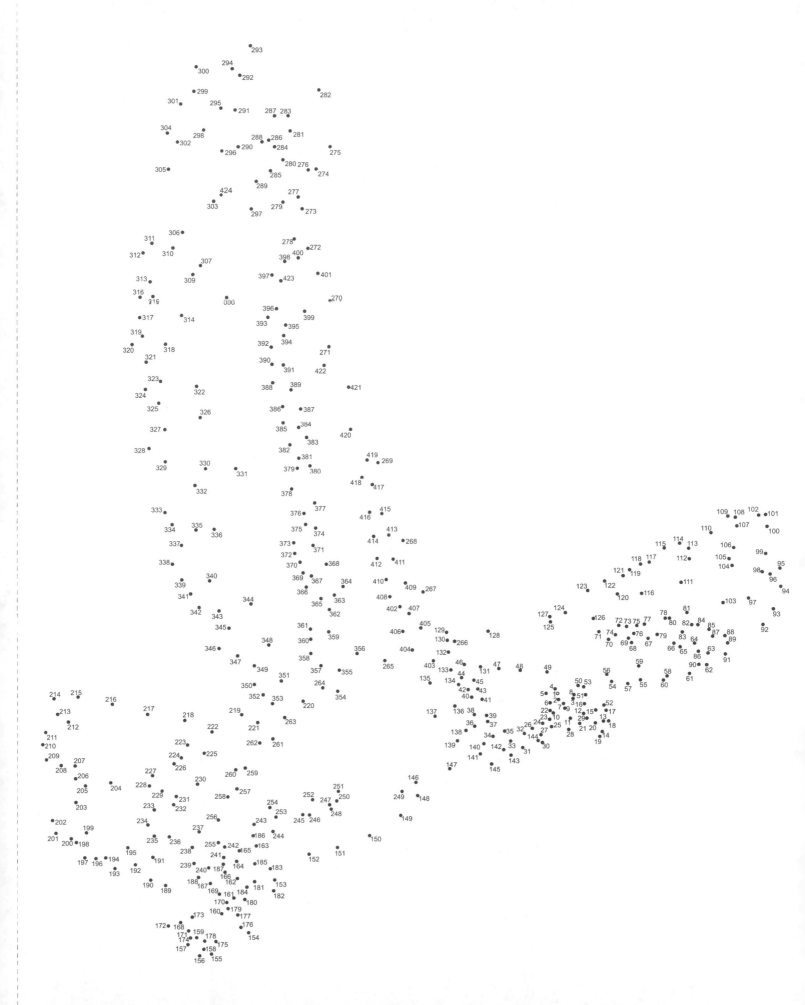

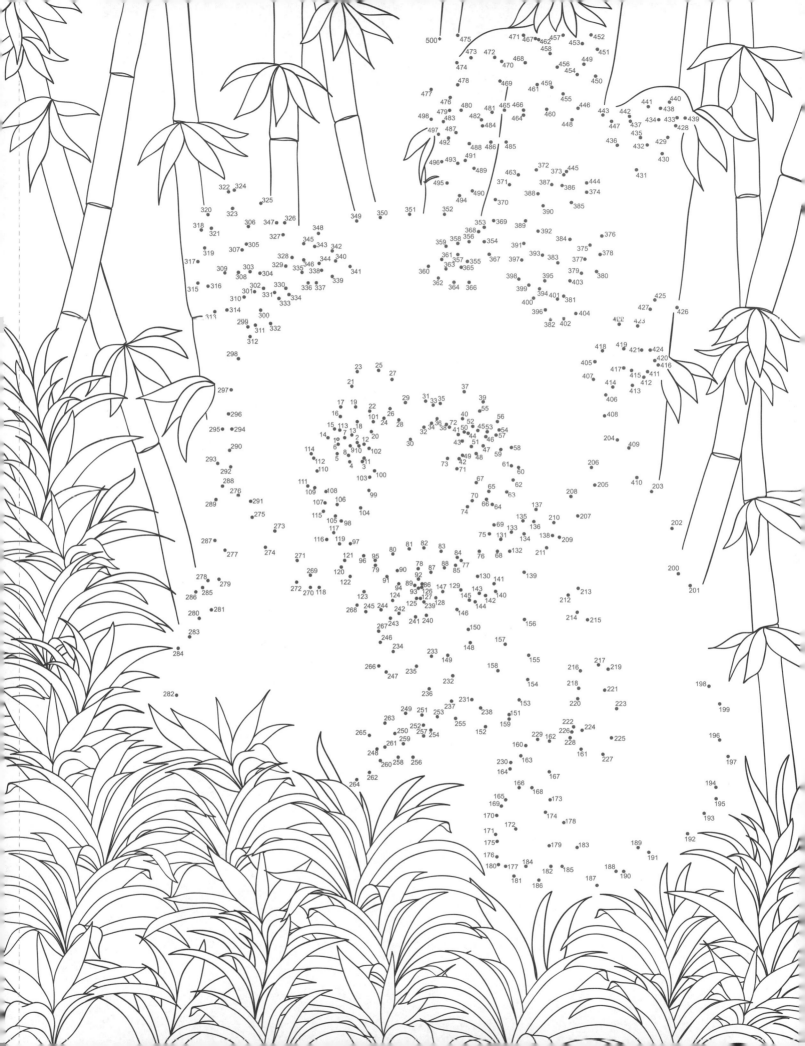

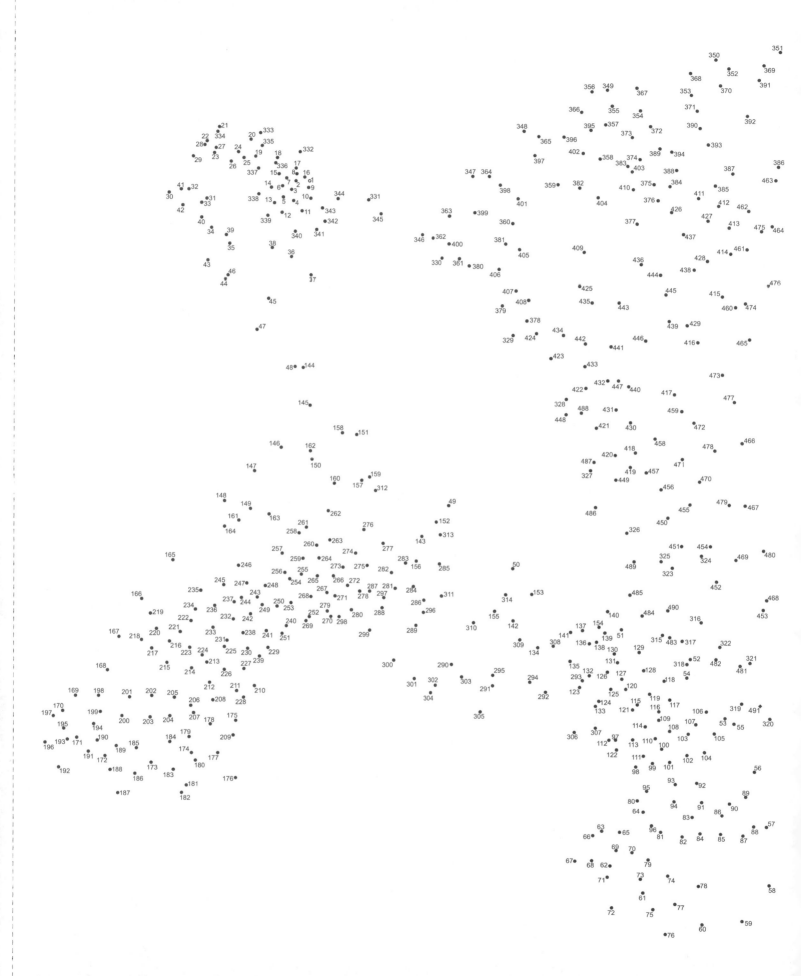

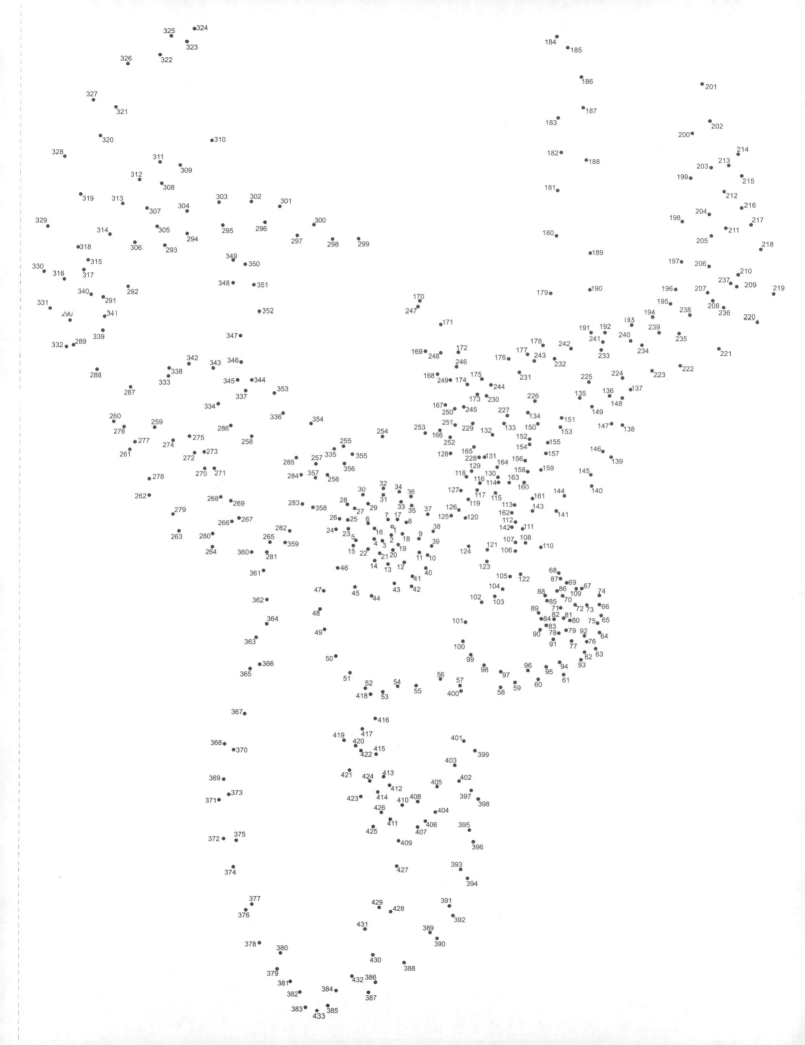

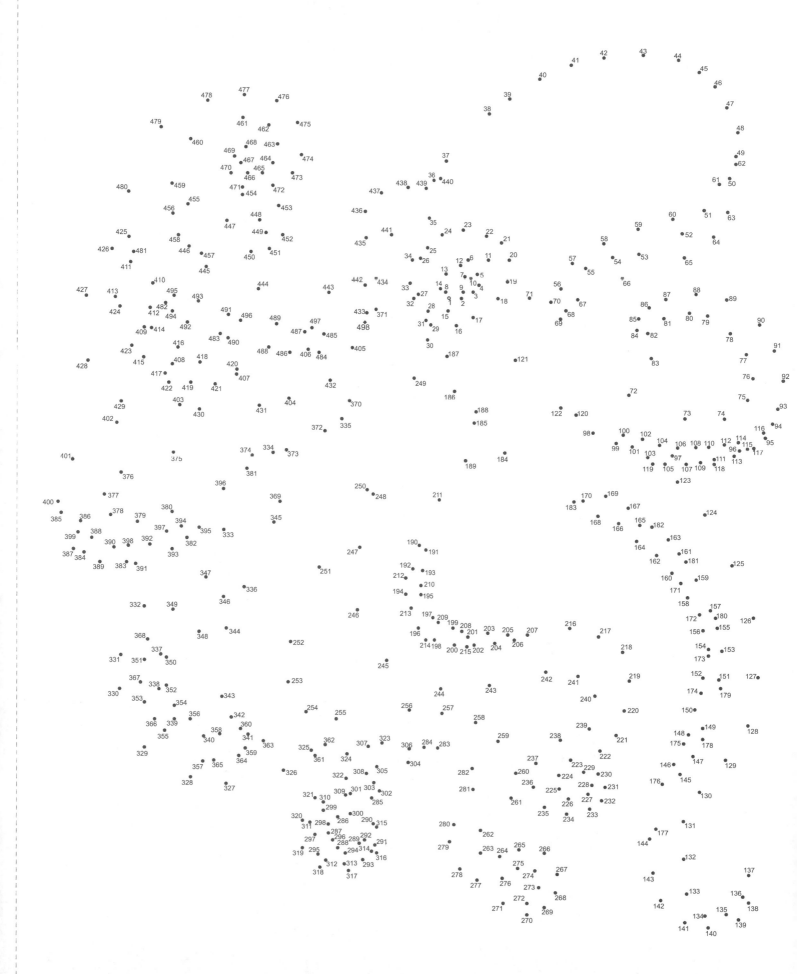

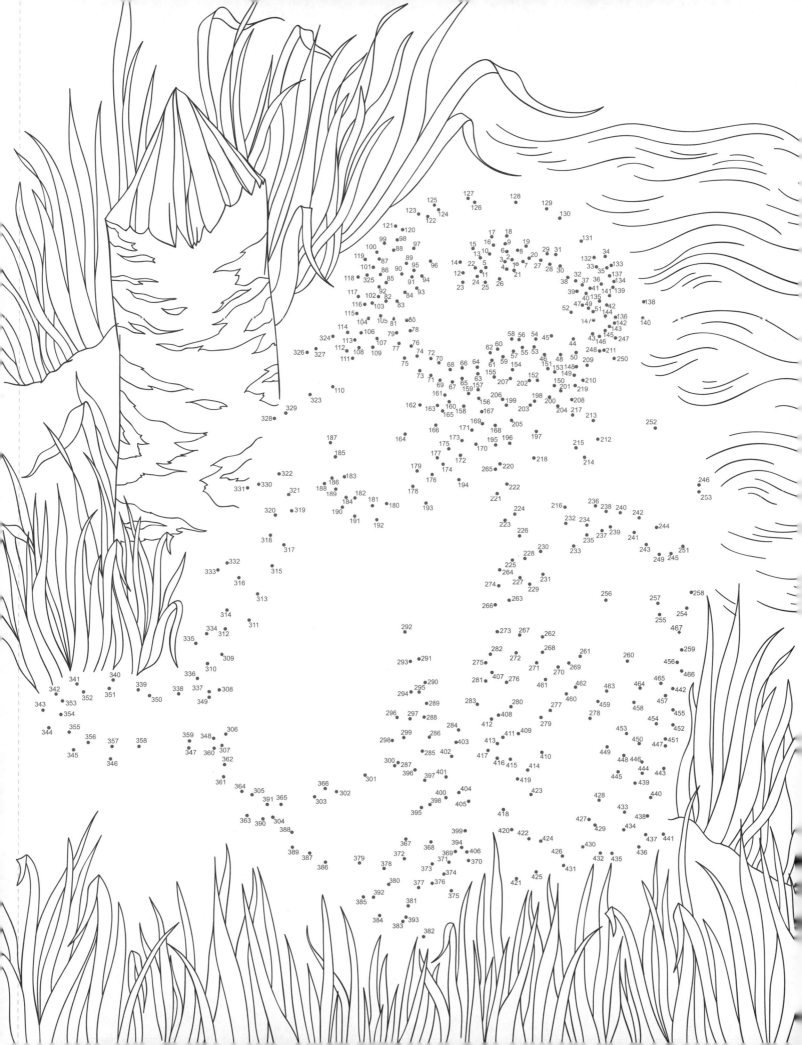

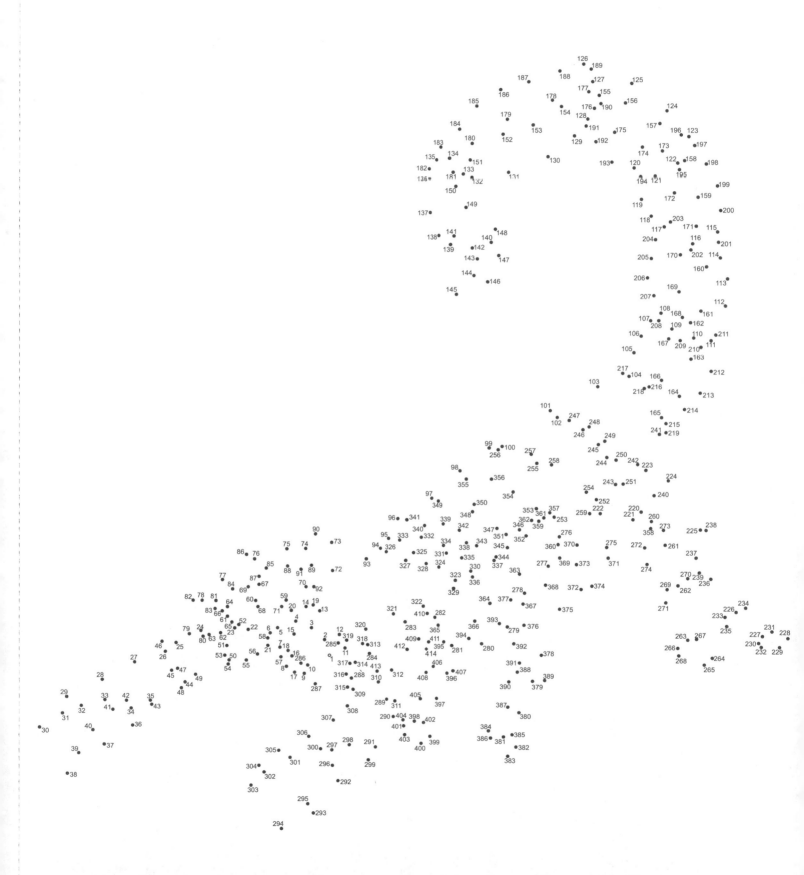

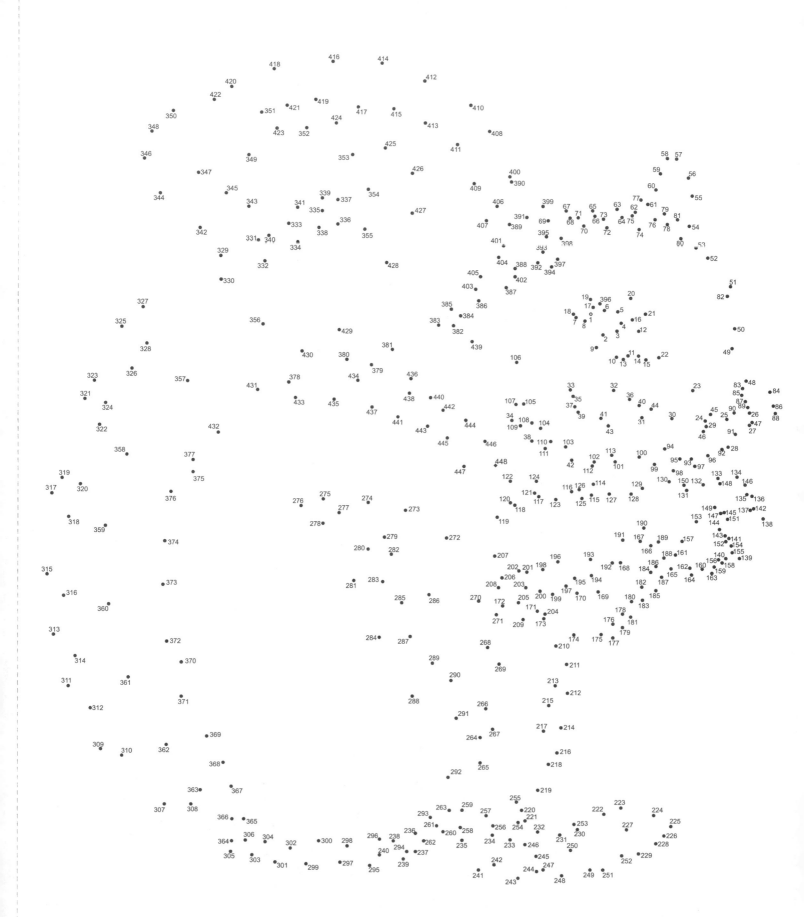

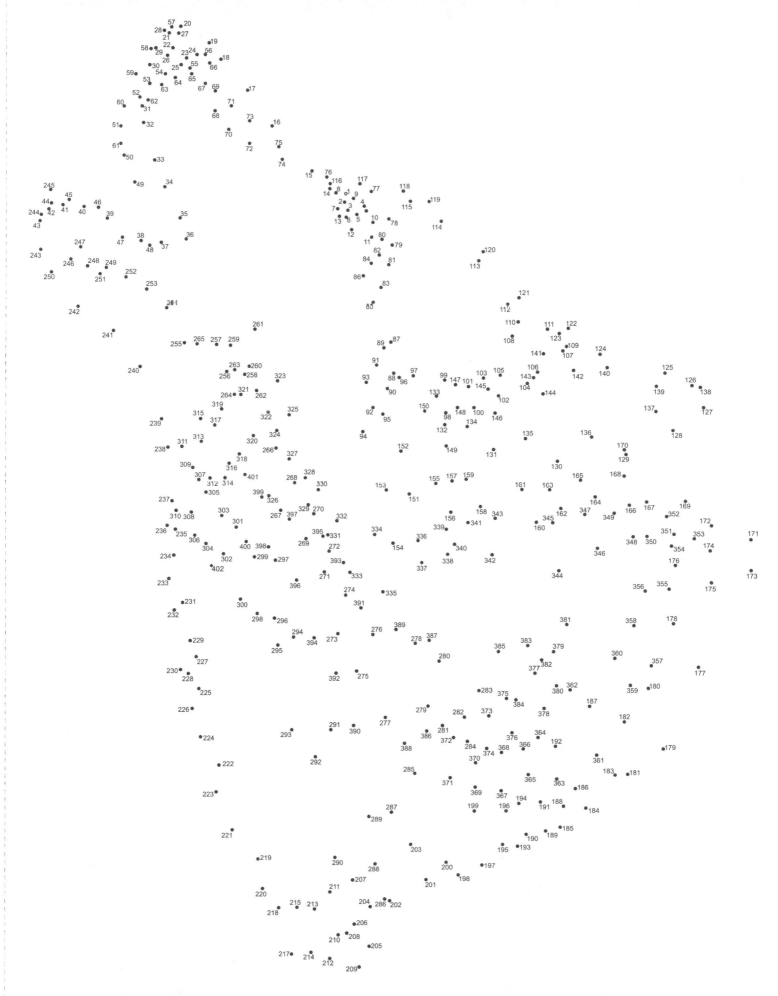

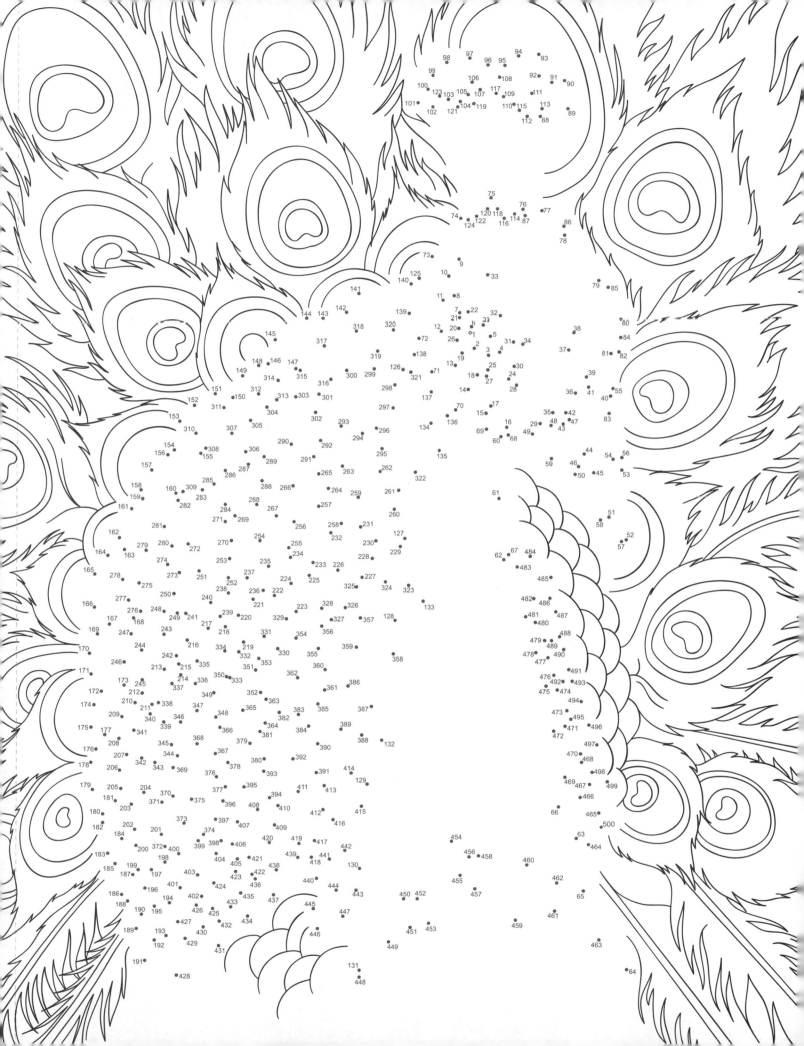

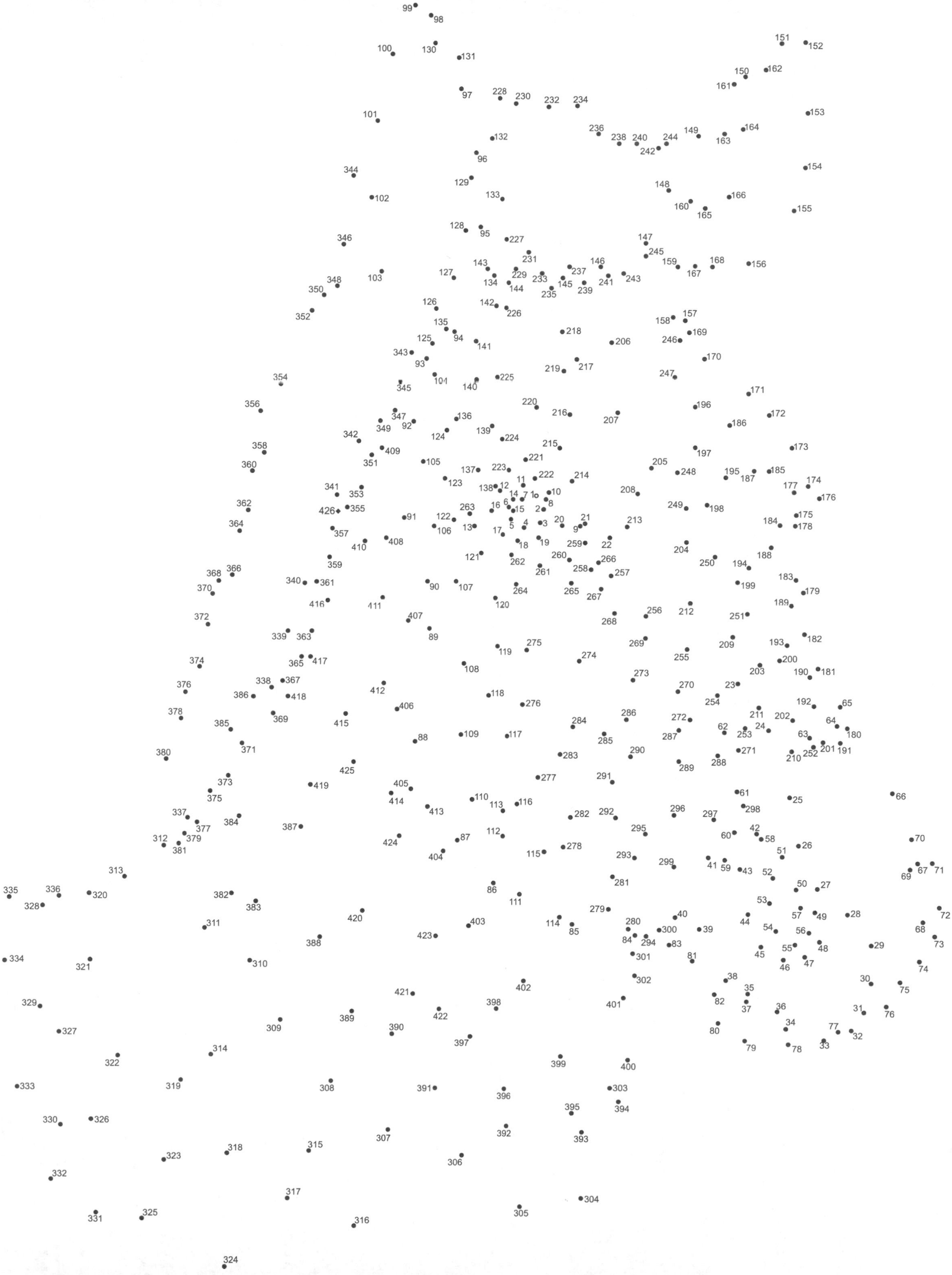

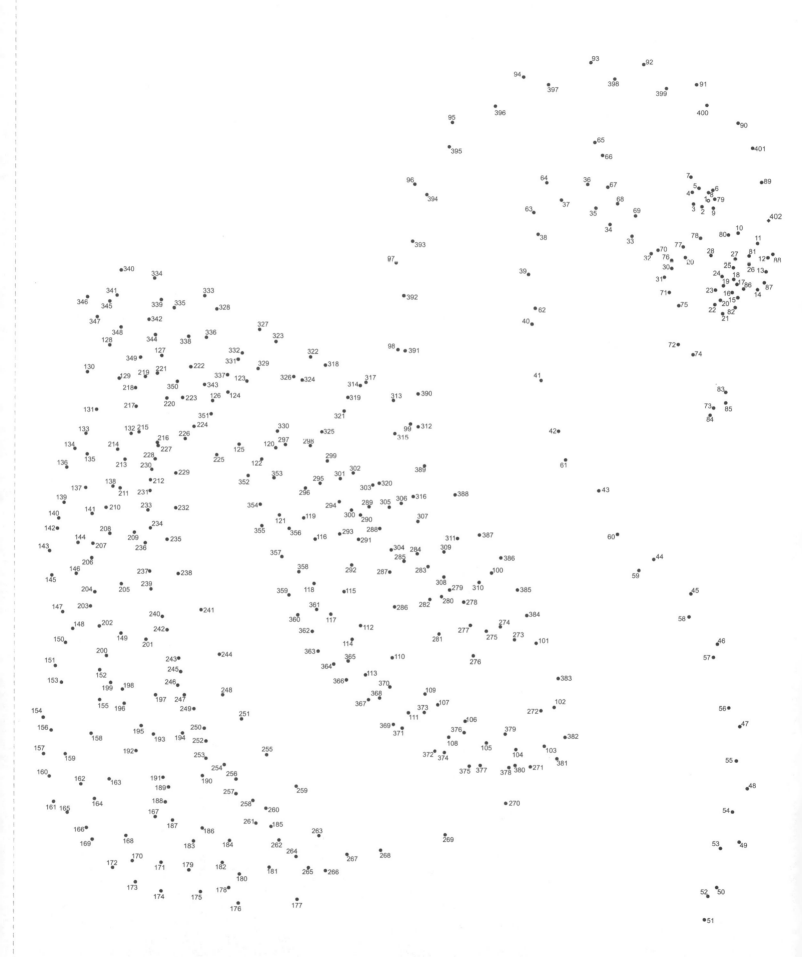

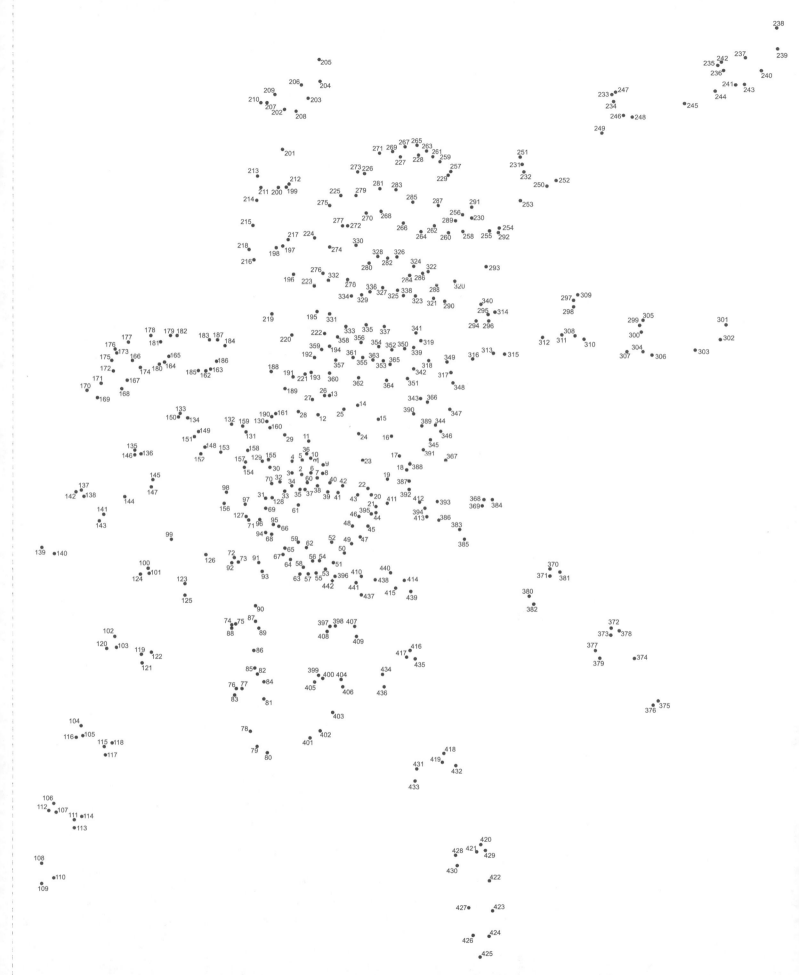

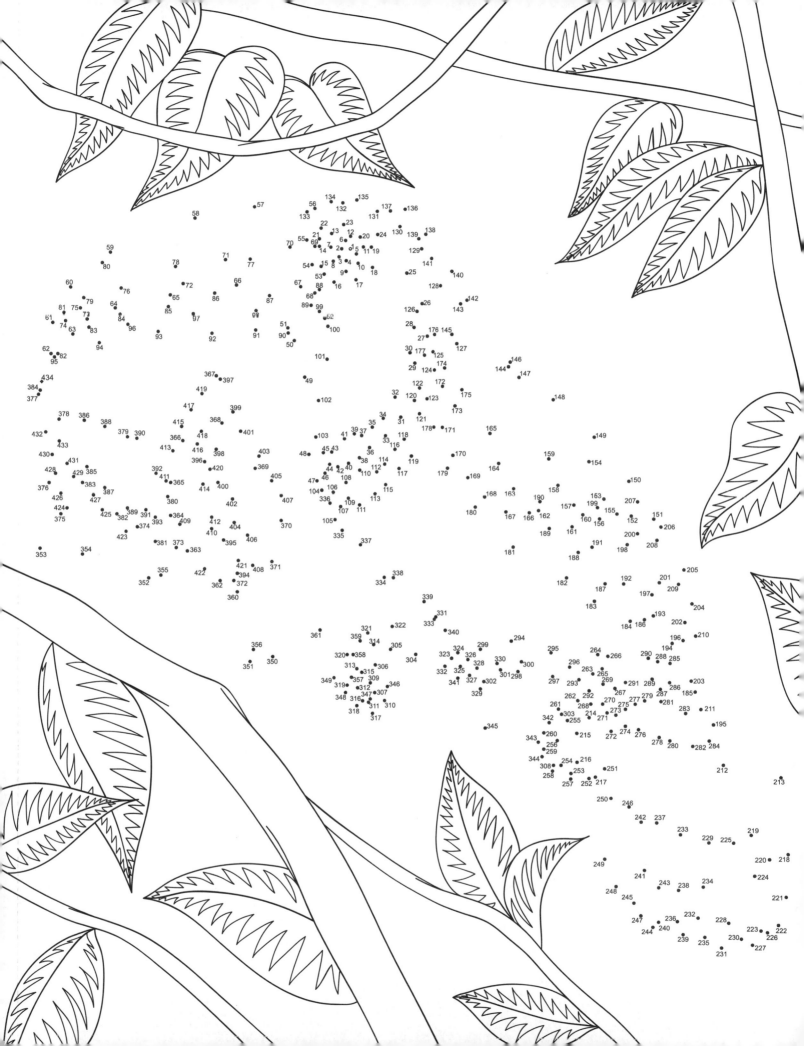

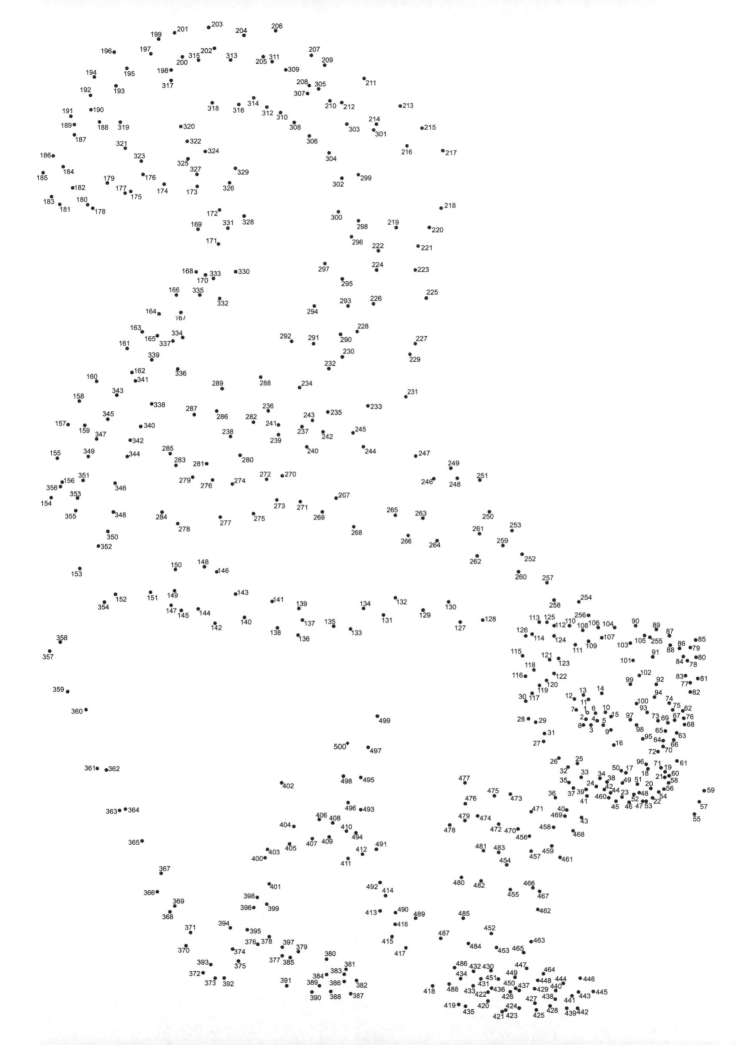

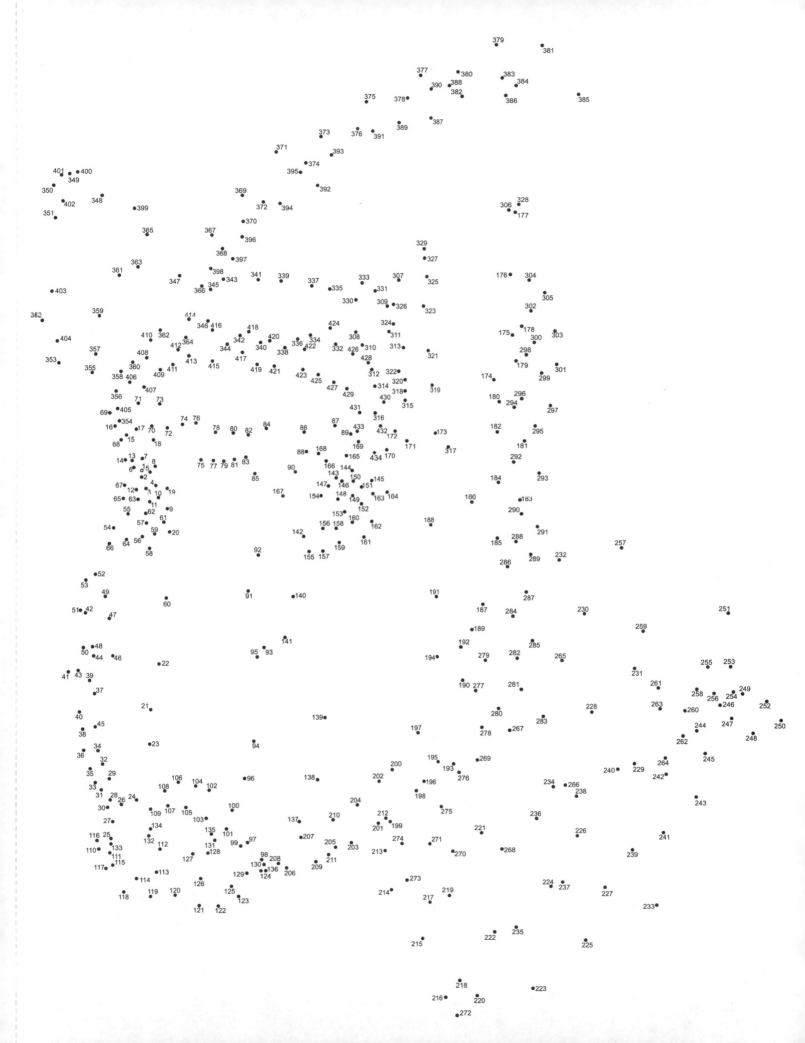

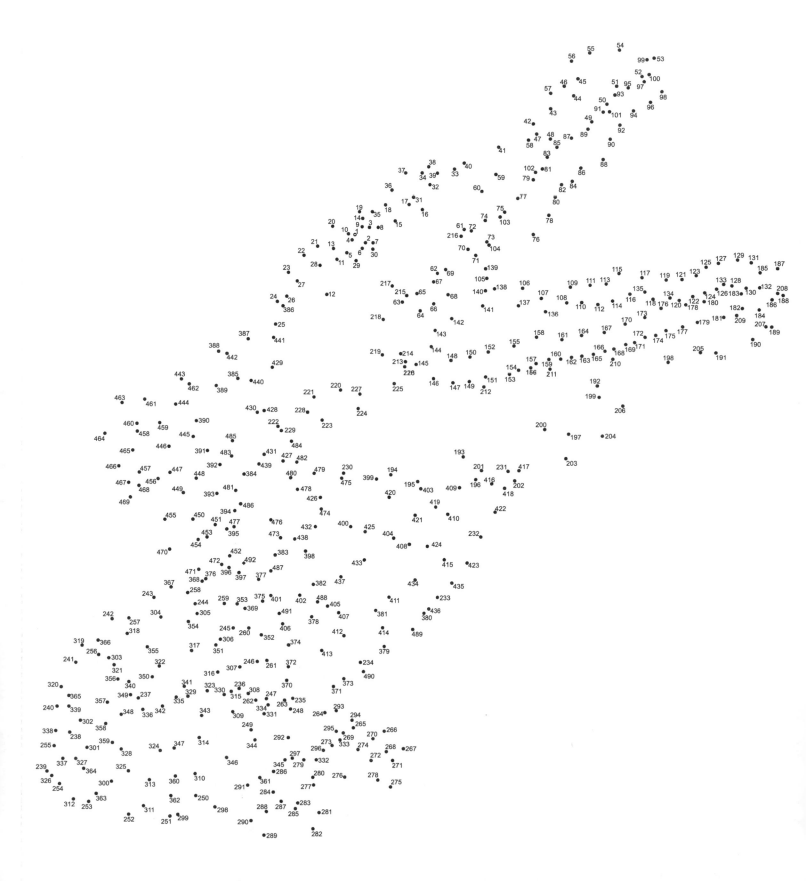

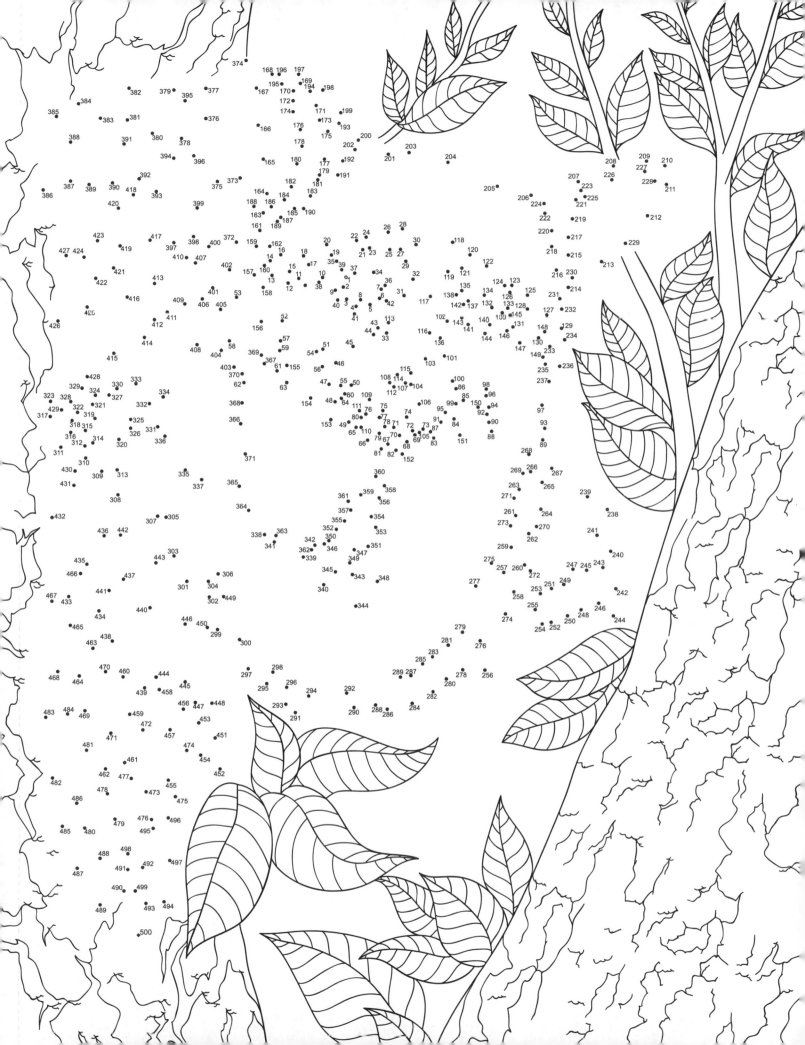

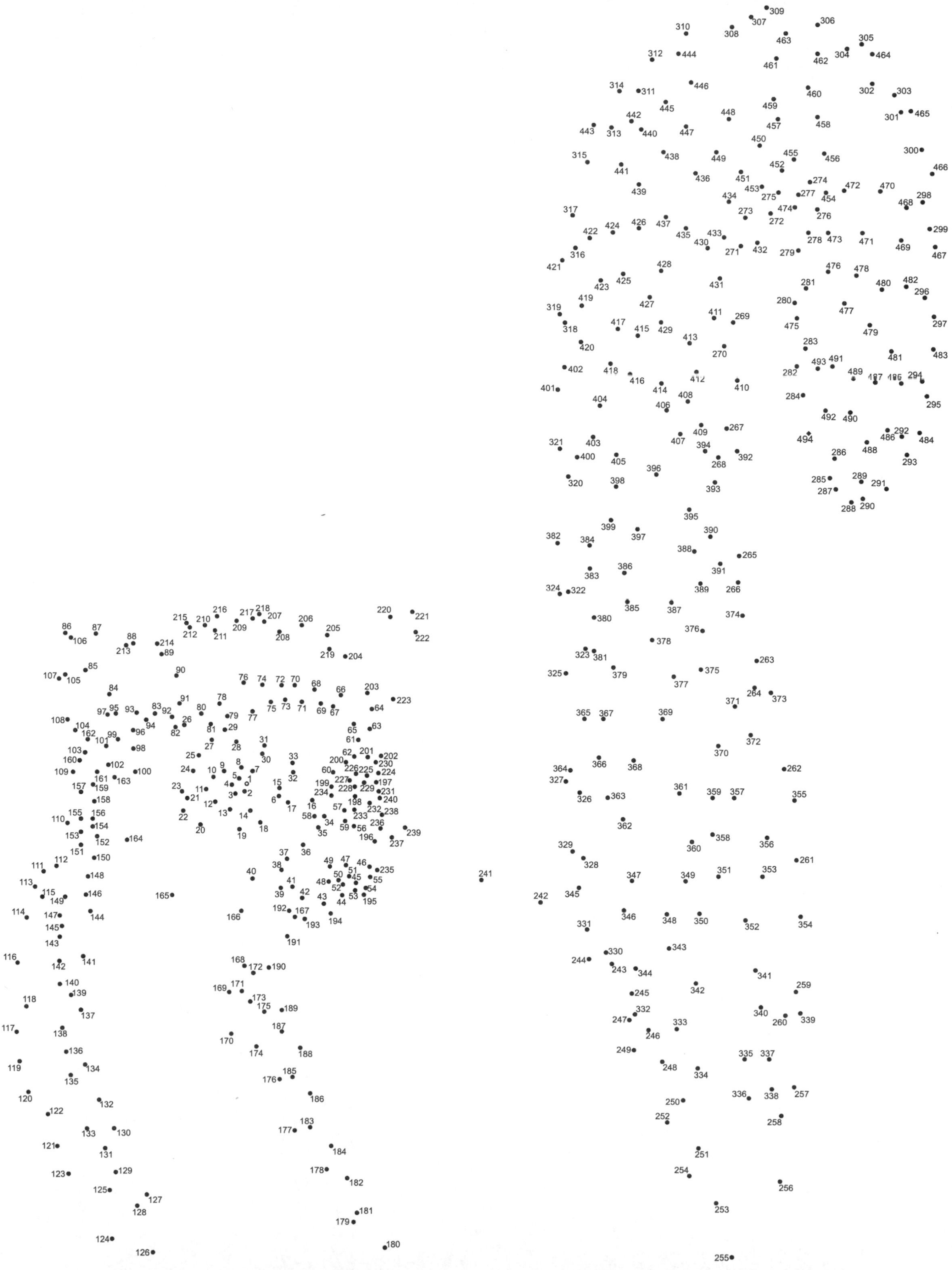

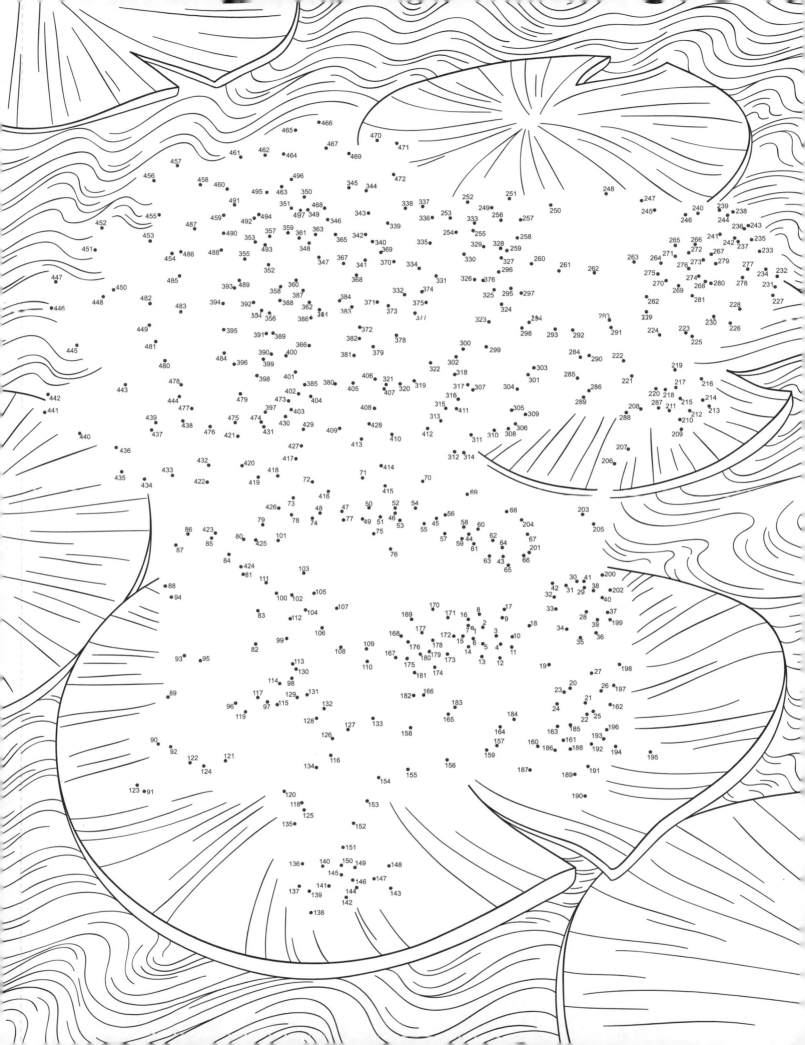

ANSWER KEY

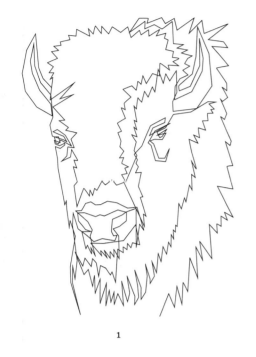

1

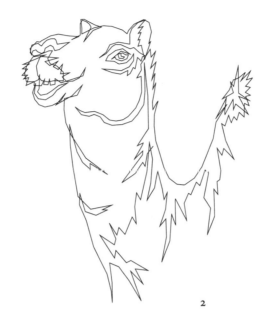

2

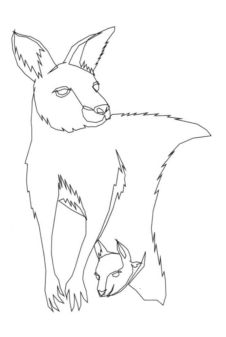

3

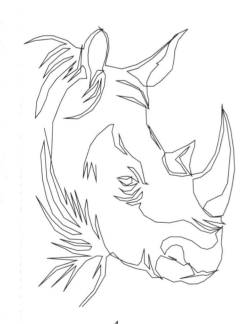

4

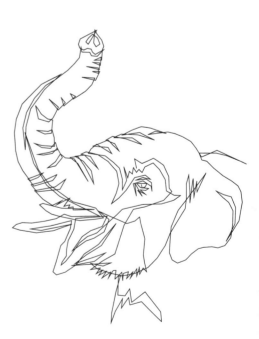

5

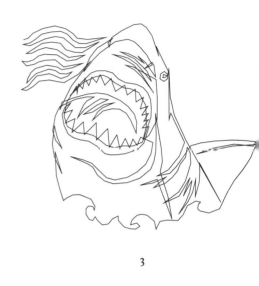

6

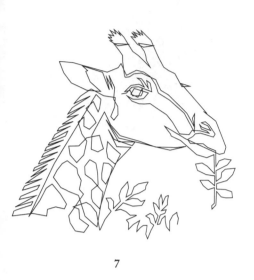

7

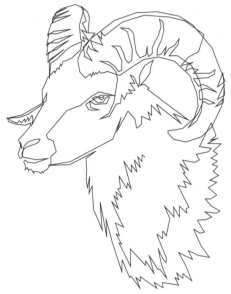

8

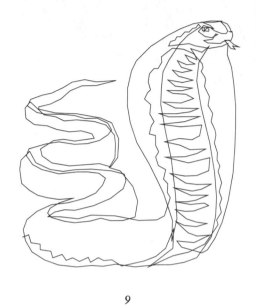

9

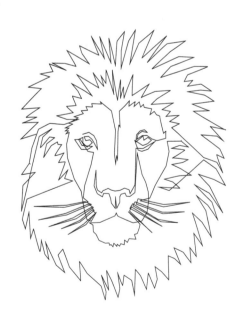

10

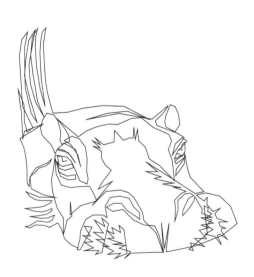

11

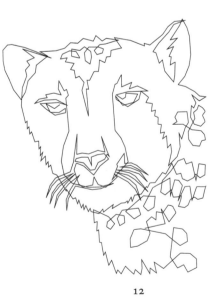

12

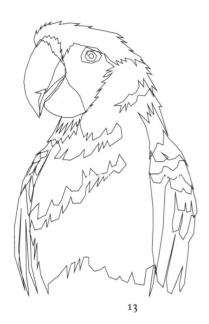

13

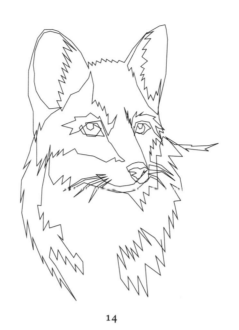

14

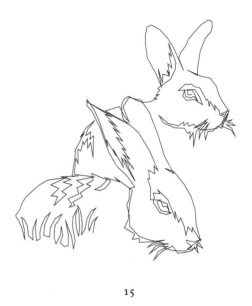

15

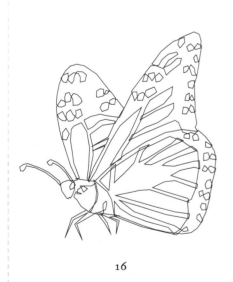

16

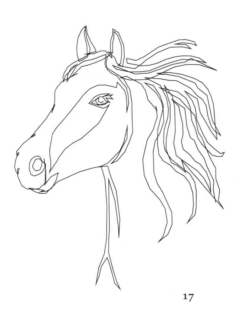

17

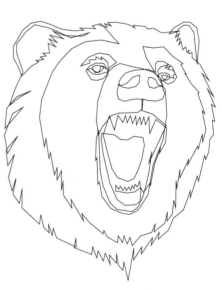

18

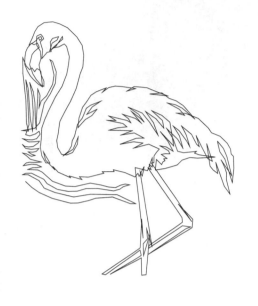

19

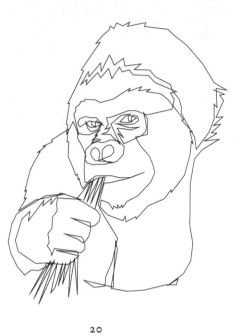

20

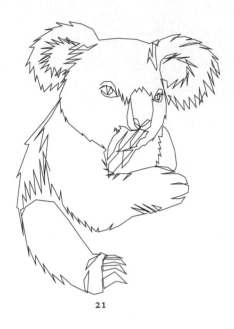

21

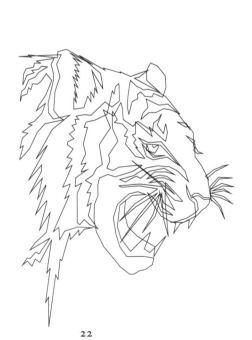

22

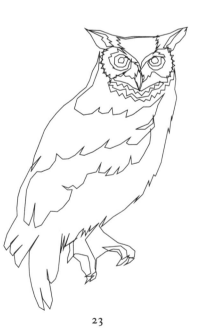

23

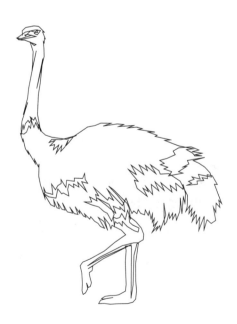

24

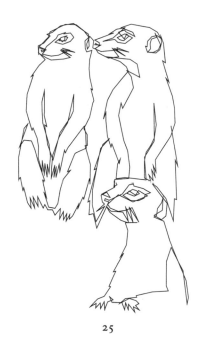

25

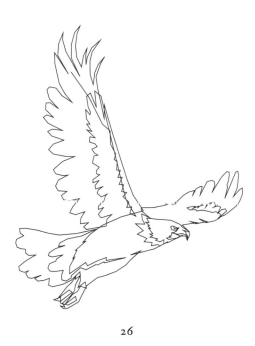

26

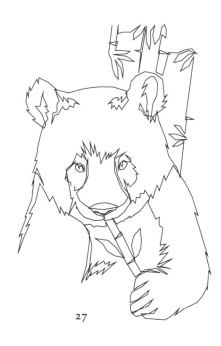

27

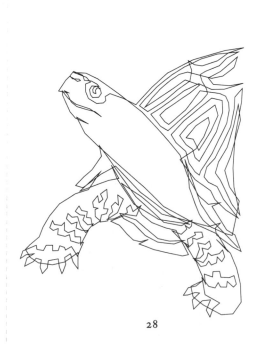

28

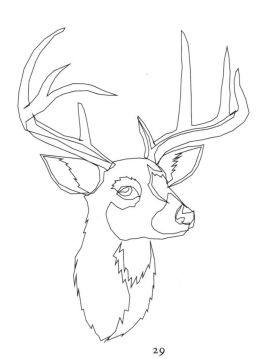

29

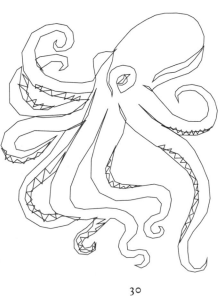

30

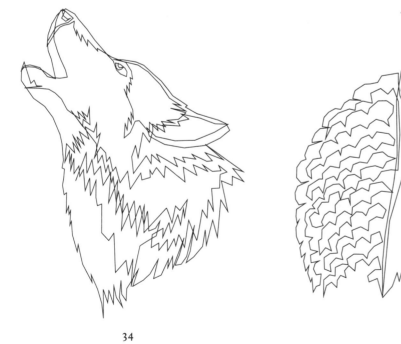

31

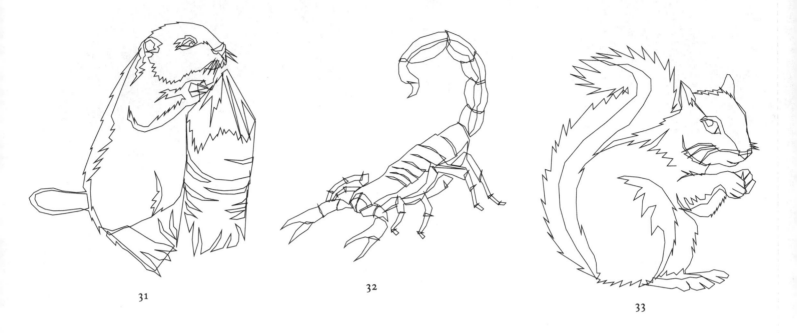

32

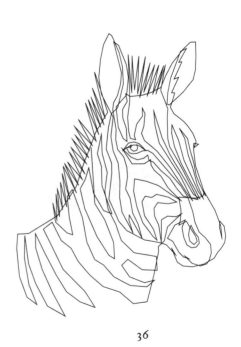

33

34

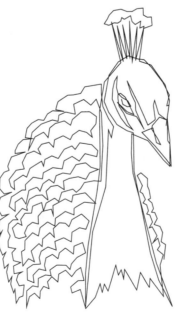

35

36

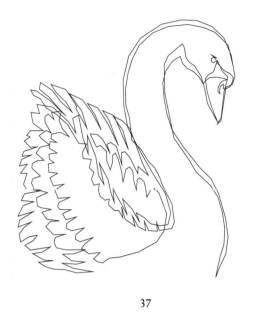

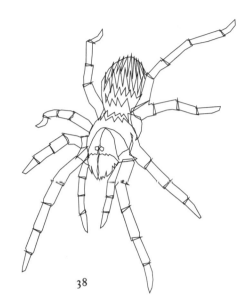

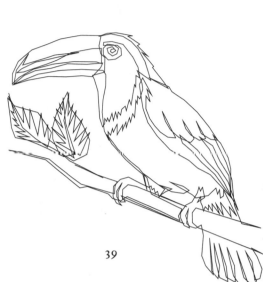

37

38

39

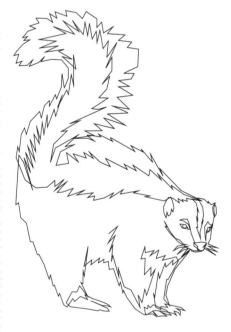

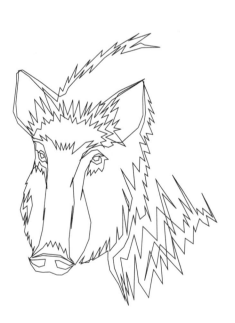

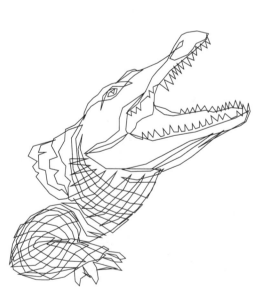

40

41

42

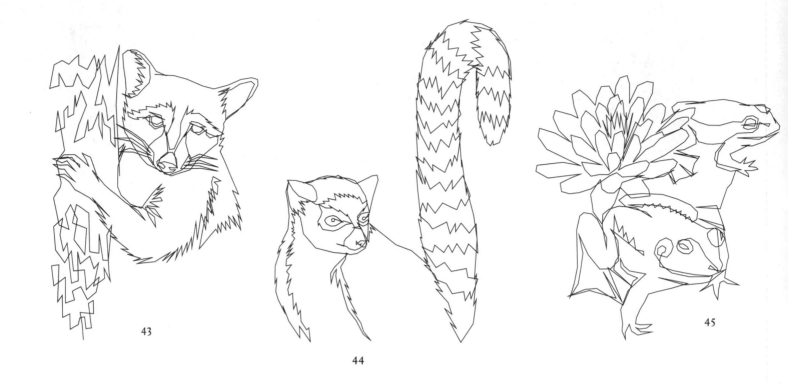

43

44

45